BUYING MORE HOUSE

for LESS MONEY

How to Make Sure You Get Your Money's Worth

Ceil Lohmar

PROBUS PUBLISHING COMPANY
Chicago, Illinois

Library of Congress Cataloging-in-Publication Data

Lohmar, Ceil.
   Buying more house for less money : how to make sure you get your
money's worth / Ceil Lohmar.
        p.   cm.
   Includes index.
   ISBN 1-55738-162-3 : $9.95
   1. House buying. 2. Real estate business. I. Title
HD1379.L6465 1990
643'.12—dc20   90-47656
                                                                     CIP

Printed in the United States of America

BP

1   2   3   4   5   6   7   8   9   0

CONTENTS

INTRODUCTION

Today, if you're a cost-conscious buyer, you can shop wisely and find ways to save money on just about anything from refrigerators to Cadillacs. But when it comes to buying a home, the largest purchase most of us will ever make, there is an iron curtain—an agent-dominated buying system—that locks us outside the action.

A buyer for an international boutique told me recently, "It's absurd. Here I am, an experienced international buyer, and I have to have an agent to help me buy a home in the town where I've lived all my life.

"I make my living buying. I have a reputation as a smart buyer. My boss, the boutique owner, says the shop's success is due to my talent for sniffing out bargains.

"I work alone. That's important. I travel the world alone. I buy merchandise from shops in Paris, Hong Kong, London. You name it, I've been there. And I get there on airline tickets I buy at bargain rates—alone. But back home? I can't buy a place to live without help.

"An agent? Frankly, I don't want an agent. I want a tour guide, someone familiar with home buying. The home market is like a strange, foreign island within an otherwise familiar country. I want to know the customs and the basic words to communicate clearly. When I know that, I can do what I do best—be my own expert, cut out the middlemen, and get the lowest possible price."

These words, and this one woman's representative frustration, helped unmask for me the need for a revolution. That's why I've written this book: to outline an alternative, money-saving way to buy residential real estate.

IS THIS BOOK FOR YOU?

Don't be misled by the simple beauty of this idea to buy a home without the help—and expense—of a real estate agent. Buying a home on your own will involve considerable time, work, and energy. Homes for sale are not lined up in parking lots like old Chevrolets; it takes a special kind of person to find them alone, but the rewards can be great.

Do it alone and you can:

- Save on the real estate commission fee, which averages 6 to 7 percent of the total purchase price.

- Compare financing and price on *your* terms— according to what's important to *you*.

- Judge homes—without pressure—according to how they might "fit" *your* way of living, *your* family and household.

- Open your field of viewing as wide as *you* wish—free of influence from stuffy stereotypes and pre-cast molds that tell you, this is how you do it, "this is where you belong."

- Look at *all* homes for sale—those sold by agents and by owners, even people who are thinking about selling but haven't put their property on the market. You won't be limited to just those homes included in the multiple listing service on which real estate agents rely almost exclusively.

But know, too, what this challenge will require of you:

- Grit, gumption, and a willingness to play a different game of buying—more entrepreneur-like.
- Curiosity. It takes wonderment, a sense of excitement in the unknown and a delight in discovery to explore all the home-buying options open to you.
- Care and gentleness. Homes for sale are generally still occupied by the owners. Respect for the household, courtesy, consideration, and good manners are essential.
- Openness. If you share with friends and family that you are looking for a home to buy, your chance of finding the place you want multiplies.

Consider the conclusion of my conversation with the frustrated international buyer:

Ceil: What is your first problem with buying a home?

Buyer: Finding homes for sale. I'm sure there are homes out there for sale, but I don't know how to find them.

Ceil: Do you answer classified ads in newspapers and go to open houses?

Buyer: Yes, but there are too few. And with most of them an agent opens the door. I know that real estate agents are no different from the middlemen in the foreign markets in which I deal. If there is an agent, no matter that the sellers pay the agent's fee, that extra cost will

	be included in the price I pay. I might not know how much is actually paid, but I do know that in the end, I, the buyer, have paid a fee for services that I could have done without.
Ceil:	How do you get around that when you're dealing in the foreign markets?
Buyer:	I represent myself and I only buy bargains. That means cutting out those costly middlemen.
Ceil:	In foreign countries, how do you find merchandise that you want to buy?
Buyer:	Before I enter a country, I learn something about it. Specifically, I learn the customs. I learn to deal in that country's money. I learn some basic words in that country's language.
Ceil:	Customs, money, and basic words; knowing these things is what opens these markets for you, right?
Buyer:	Absolutely.
Ceil:	The same holds true for home buying. Perhaps nothing is stranger in American culture than the multiple listing system that real estate companies have developed. Real estate companies don't compete. They don't uphold the old American tradition of finding ways to provide a better product at a better price than the other guys. Real estate companies cooperate with each other. They band together like the foreign oil-producing countries do in OPEC, and their ways are foreign to most buyers. You'll need to know the customs of the real estate industry.
Buyer:	OK. I see that. But doesn't an agent help you borrow money, too? I don't understand mortgages and all that.

Ceil: You're not alone. The mortgage game is strange to just about everyone. But you can learn to shop for bargains in mortgages, too. Since the deregulation of the banking industry, competition is wide open in mortgaging, just like air fares. And you don't need a real estate agent to act as an intermediary. You can deal directly with any mortgage lender you want.

Buyer: One thing I know about mortgages is the cost for interest on the money I will borrow. Are there other costs?

Ceil: Yes. There are up-front costs that you must pay before you get the money. Here, shopping smart really makes a difference. You'll find there are some significant differences in the costs of borrowing money from different lenders. By knowing what you're doing and shopping around, you can find the borrowing plan that is best for you.

Buyer: OK. I believe I can be my own real estate agent, learn to find homes for sale, and shop the mortgage market. If you give me a list of the important home-buying words, am I ready to start looking?

Ceil: Just one more thing—legal matters. How do you handle legal issues in your work?

Buyer: I don't touch them. I leave the legal matters to a lawyer. Local laws vary and they change often.

Ceil: That's exactly what I recommend when buying a home. Leave the legal documentation to a legal authority. The fee you'll pay is small considering the major problems a lawyer, an escrow agent, or title agent, can help you avoid.

Buyer: It sounds like, just as it is with my work, to get the best deal you have to run your own show. My years of experience buying goods all over the world has taught me that smart buying takes three talents: knowing good merchandise; knowing a good price and where to cut corners; and knowing how to watch out for yourself. The ancient code for buying is alive and well—Buyer Beware!

Ceil: And the modern postscript is Buyer Be Smart!

If these feelings and problems sound similar to your situation, read on. *Buy More Home for Less Money* will 1) help give you the knowledge and the confidence you need to buy a home on your own, 2) help you learn how to find a home that really fills your needs and expectations, and 3) teach you how you can save some money in the process.

WORKING THE MULTIPLE-LISTING SYSTEM FOR DISCOUNTS

To work the system, any system, you first must know how it operates. Step 1 will give you an inside look at how the real estate business functions and specific instructions about how to make it work in your favor. I'll show you how to:

- WATCH WHERE YOUR MONEY GOES

- BE INDEPENDENT AND ASK FOR THE DISCOUNT

- EXERCISE YOUR BUYING FREEDOMS

- USE THE REQUEST FOR AN AGENT'S FEE DISCOUNT FORM

- HAND THE REQUEST TO EACH AGENT

- STAND UP TO THE MULTIPLE-LISTING AGENT

- TEST TRUE COLORS OF AN AGENT

- SEEK OUT THE SELLER'S AGENT

- KNOCK ON THE SELLER'S DOOR

- CALCULATE THE DOLLARS YOU DISCOUNT

- LEARN BASIC AGENCY WORDS

WATCH WHERE YOUR MONEY GOES

If you're looking for a deal on a home, the most critical thing to remember is that—in our agent-dominated real estate system—home buyers make their own discounts.

The traditional home transaction—where the buyer enlists the aid of a multiple listing service agent—primarily involves four people: the buyer, the seller, and the seller's and buyer's agents. Each of the four walks away from the table carrying receipts after finalizing a deal. The receipts are simple, but they tell an interesting story: The buyer pays everyone. They read this way:

BUYER'S RECEIPT:

Price Paid for Home	$80,000

SELLER'S RECEIPT:

Received from Buyer	$80,000
Paid to Seller's Agent	– $ 4,800
(as per terms of listing contract)	
Price to Seller for Home	$75,200

SELLER'S AGENT'S RECEIPT:

Received from Seller	$ 4,800
Split with Buyer's Agent	
(50% of $4,800)	– $ 2,400
Seller's Agent's Fee	$ 2,400

BUYER'S AGENT'S RECEIPT:

Fee Split from Seller's Agent	$ 2,400

The receipts tell more:

The buyer paid $4,800 more for the home than the seller was willing to accept. The buyer will move into a home for which he or she paid $80,000 that was worth $75,200 to the seller.

There is a possible conflict of interest for the buyer's agent. Splitting fees from the seller's side while appearing to be on the buyer's side cannot help but create situations of mixed loyalties. Did the buyer know that his or her agent would cost $2,400 cash at closing? Was the agent's service worth $2,400? Would the buyer have agreed to pay $2,400 cash directly to the seller's agent? Without expecting to be paid directly by the buyer, did that buyer's agent work to get the lowest price for the buyer? Or, knowing that the buyer was in the dark about the fees, did the agent merely take the quickest route to a commission fee?

It's puzzling. The seller, the seller's agent, and the buyer's agent all leave with some of the buyer's money. The buyer leaves with 30 years indebtedness to a mortgage company and with considerably less cash.

A lawyer once used a courtroom analogy to explain the oddities of this suspicious business to me. He said, "A buyer in a multiple listing network purchase is like a defendant going into court expecting to be defended by the prosecuting attorney."

Q. Do buyers often ask about their agent's fees?

A. No, not that I've seen. In my years selling homes, only one buyer ever asked about my fee. This buyer was from Holland and in that country, he explained, buyers and sellers, by law, must have separate agents. Buyers and sellers must pay their agents directly. Agents cannot split fees.

Q. What's the difference between a realtor, an agent, and a broker?

A. An agent and a broker are licensed by the state. If they join the local trade association—the Board of Realtors—they also become realtors.

BE INDEPENDENT AND ASK FOR THE DISCOUNT

If you are a cost-conscious buyer, you're accustomed to buying everything independently; everything, that is, with the probable exception of real estate. Although you may have never considered it until now, you can also be independent in buying a home. You can act as your own agent and, as a result, negotiate with sellers and the sellers agent for a discount of the buyers agents fee. But you have to ask for the discount.

It's a giant step to be an independent home buyer, but it can save you money in a giant way.

Q. What exactly does a real estate agent do?

A. A real estate license allows an agent to bring together a buyer and seller of a property and help them negotiate a price. More than that—such as advising on the law, investment, and income taxes—is a "no-no."

Q. Buying my home is the biggest investment in my life. Am I wise to buy one on my own?

A. Yes, you are wise to do everything except the legal documentation. When you are prepared to sign a legally binding sales contract, have a lawyer or escrow agent take over. Even if you hire a real estate agent, taking title to a home without a legal expert is too risky. But on your own you can find a home you love, make a low offer on it, and reach an agreement with the seller about price, financing, and possession date. After all, it's your home, your nest, your haven from the world. It's your money. You earned it, you saved it. Whose judgment can you trust better than your own? Surely not that of an agent who is paid by the seller's agent.

Being independent will not only save you the buyer's agent's fee. (The statement Request For Buyers Agent's Fee Discount is on page 13.) Being independent allows you freedom to pursue home's for sale by agents and by the owners themselves; to make low offers; and to negotiate a price without prejudice, opinions, or steering.

EXERCISE YOUR BUYING FREEDOM

Q. What is meant by a free market?

A. In a free market anyone can buy or sell. Further, it means that prices are not fixed or predetermined by an outside party. The price is whatever a buyer and a seller agree to at a given time. Real estate is bought and sold in a free-market environment.

Q. Isn't a license required for me to buy independently?

A. No, a license is not required. If you want to collect a fee for helping a friend buy a home, you better have a license. But for yourself, you're free to buy your own home as freely as you buy your own shoes.

USE THE REQUEST FOR THE BUYER'S AGENT'S FEE DISCOUNT

It will take nerve, but you can negotiate with sellers and real estate agents for agent's fees discounts. On the next few pages are tools to help you.

First is the important Request For Buyer's Agent's Fee Discount.

Second is a suggested script to use when you hand the Discount form to each agent you meet. Use the form and the script to claim your independence and ask for a discount on your first step into a home being sold by a real estate company.

Third is a list of answers to questions asked frequently about negotiating discounts.

HAND THE REQUEST TO EACH AGENT

Here's a sample script of how you want your first encounter with each real estate agent to transpire:

You: Hi. I'm interested in the home you're showing, but I'd like you to read this before I look at the property.

Agent: What is it?

You: Is this home multiple-listed?

Agent: Yes.

You: Well, this is my claim to represent myself and a request for a discount in the fee that the seller would be obligated to pay to the buyer's agent.

Agent: Ah, you don't have to worry about that fee; the seller takes care of that. The seller's listing

REQUEST FOR BUYER'S AGENT'S FEE DISCOUNT

I am an independent buyer. If I buy a multiple-listed home, I will disclaim the claim of any agent to represent me or to claim the buyer's agent's split of the real estate fee.

Further, I will only sign a sales contract that states: Since there is no buyer's agent, the seller's agent agrees to reduce the obligation of the seller to pay the real estate fee by the amount usually paid to the buyer's agent.

Date ___*March 1, 1990*___

Buyer's signature ___*Phillip Dominick*___

	contract obliges the seller to pay the fee for the seller's agent and the buyer's agent.
You:	You mean that the real estate agent's fees are built into the selling price. Isn't that right?
Agent:	Well, yes.
You:	Then, if we're being honest, we can see that the buyer really pays the fees.
Agent:	I don't look at it that way.
You:	I do, I have to. I honor the seller's right to choose to be represented by an agent. However, I expect the same right to choose. I choose not to have an agent and to represent myself. So it follows, if I buy a home where the seller has committed to paying a fee which will be split between agents, I can logically request a discount of the buyer's agent's fee.
Agent:	You can't do that.
You:	Yes, I can. Look at it this way. If I have a signed contract with a buyer's agent to represent me, will you pay the fee to that agent?
Agent:	Yes. We'll do that. Our company will pay the fee to whomever you designate.
You:	Let me be sure I'm getting that right. Your company will pay the buyer's agent's split of the fee to whomever I designate. Is that right?
Agent:	Yes, that's right.
You:	I designate no one. And since there is no buyer's agent, I would expect that the seller's agent could reduce the fee charged the seller by the amount of fee that would have been paid to the buyer's agent.

STAND UP TO THE MULTIPLE-LISTING AGENT

Q. In your experience, how have sellers' agents responded to requests for discounts on buyers' agents' fees?

A. They have agreed to it. I've heard agents say to sellers, "I'll go along with the discount. It's fine with me. It's just as though there were a buyer's agent. I get exactly what I expected."

Q. Why should I specify a discount in the real estate fee? Why not just offer the seller a low price?

A. Because you want the sellers to accept your offer. You want the offer to give the *sellers* the most money. By reducing the amount that the sellers have to pay agents, you raise the amount the sellers can keep for themselves. For example, if you make a low offer of $70,000 without the discount, then the sellers have to pay $4,200 in fees and can net for themselves only $65,800.

But if you request the discount, the sellers pay only $2,100 in fees and net for themselves $67,800. Sure, you pay the same, but the offer is more tempting for the sellers.

Q. Why can't I just ask the seller's agent for the discount?

A. You can. But because the sellers and the listing agent have a signed contract for that fee, you have to be sure that the seller knows that he or she—the seller—gets the discount. Make sure the seller knows the benefit to himself or herself in discounting the fee.

Q. What incentive is there for the seller's agent to agree to give me the discount?

A. Fairness, sense of honor, ethics, good will, and the improved prospects for making a sale. After all, there is no buyer's agent in your case to claim the fee split.

Q. Are agents concerned about reputations? Would the agent be afraid to look greedy saying to sellers, "True, there is in this offer no buyer's agent's claim to a split of the fee as is usual. But we have a contract for you to pay me 6 percent and I'll hold you to it. I won't budge. You pay me as we agree, and I will keep the whole fee myself"?

A. Certainly, agents are concerned about reputation. If you were a seller (with an offer from a buyer asking for a discount) and your agent responded as above, wouldn't you say the agent was greedy?

Q. As an independent buyer, how will I go about making an offer?

A. You can use the offer form on page 84. This is an easy, flexible, inexpensive way to come to an agreement with the sellers. However, I don't recommend you sign a sales contract without legal advice. So, to save money, you can come to terms with the seller on the items covered on the Offer—price, financing, and discount of the fee. Then have a lawyer write a full, legal sales contract.

Q. If the seller's agent offers to write a legally binding sales contract should I say OK?

A. You can. But don't sign it. *Never* sign a legally binding sales contract without *your* lawyer giving the nod to go ahead.

Q. Who, seller or seller's agent, should I talk to when I want to make an offer?

A. In most cases, you'll only know the seller's agent, so you have to call the agent. If you know the seller, call and say you want to make the offer directly to them. If the sellers want their agent present, that's up to them.

Q. Can I bring a friend for support?

A. Sure. A friend can come in handy to confer with. Maybe your friend will do some of the talking. One rule: *Never allow anyone to negotiate on your behalf without you being there.*

Q. When should I go directly to the seller? Don't all offers in writing have to be presented to the seller by the seller's agent?

A. Yes, but don't take the chance that it won't be. This is too important to let out of your hands. Look after it. Be there.

Q. Is the 6 or 7 percent commission rate something the agent and the seller can renegotiate?

A. Yes. The commission fee is free and open to whatever the agent and the seller agree to.

Q. So, if the seller and the seller's agent want to change the agreement, can they?

A. Yes, but while the listing contract is in effect, they both must agree to any change before a change can take place.

Q. Do I understand correctly—there is no set fee by the board of realtors, the state, or some other powers that be?

A. That's correct. Real estate fees are negotiable for each property listed.

Q. Then why do we get the feeling that within a particular area all sellers pay the same fee? In Minneapolis people expect to pay 7 percent; in Los Angeles, 6 percent.

A. I think it's because sellers and buyers don't negotiate. Most people, even those who have used real estate services to buy or sell a home, don't know the fee is negotiable. They think they have to pay the going rate, so they don't offer to pay less.

Q. What happens in this case? I make an offer and request the buyer's agent's fee discount. The seller agrees, but the agent refuses. The agent insists on the whole fee.

A. You don't have a deal. The seller's agent can hold the seller to paying the full fee if the listing contract is still in effect. That's strictly between the seller and the seller's agent.

Q. What is the length of a listing contract?

A. Usually three to six months. They may have small print committing the seller to a longer obligation or automatic renewal. Contracts differ.

Q. When the property is multiple-listed, must I write the following statement in every sales contract? *Since there is no buyer's agent, the seller's agent agrees to reduce the obligation of the seller to pay the real estate fee by the amount usually paid to the buyer's agent.*

A. Yes. It must be stated in writing. Refuse to sign a sales contract unless that statement is in the document. You will see the reason for this when the seller and the seller's agent sign the sales contract. Once they both sign the sales contract with the statement that's it. They don't have to sign a revised listing contract. The sales contract replaces the listing contract.

Q. What if the seller's agent agrees to talk over the discount with the seller? Is that enough?

A. No. You want to state unequivocally that you won't buy unless the fee is discounted. In real estate, what is spoken does not always hold up. Put everything significant—

anything that might save you money—in writing.

OK, not every multiple listing agent will be totally cooperative. So, it's important that you are prepared to encounter all kinds. Very likely some of the homes you will want to consider will be in the multiple listing network. Unless those homes are mountaintop hideaways where the air is too rare to sustain human life, you can bet you'll meet a multiple listing agent when you get there.

Those agents want to sell homes and claim their fees. You want to buy a home, discount the fee, and lop the difference off the price. Before you venture out, know:

- In many areas, multiple listing companies have a tight grip on home sales. Figure that 99 percent of all the real estate agents selling homes are affiliated with the multiple listing network.

- The multiple listing network is composed of local units, but they are as alike as polka dots all across the country. In each, the sellers are committed to pay the whole fee if and when their homes sell. This fee is generally 6 or 7 percent of the selling price.

- The fee can be split by two agents. Roughly half to the seller's agent, half to the buyer's agent.

- Because the fee is a percentage of the selling price, the higher the selling price the higher the fee. For that reason, multiple listing agents logically tend to lean in favor of higher prices.

TEST TRUE COLORS OF AN AGENT

You're safe to assume that every agent you meet is a salesman or saleswoman for the seller. No matter how agents encourage you to make low offers, no matter how they pledge loyalty to you, question that loyalty. Face the facts. If agents are paid by the sellers, and paid more when the price is higher, they're at best a mixed bag. I think it would be a rare person in that kind of situation who would be 100 percent for you.

Here's a quick way to test an agent. If any one of the following exists, the agent is not 100 percent on your team.

- The agent works for the same company that advertises the property for sale.

- You, the buyer, have not written and signed a contract empowering that agent to work in your behalf.

- You have not agreed to pay the agent's fee.

- The fee paid to the agent is a percentage of the selling price, so that the higher the price you pay, the higher the fee the agent is paid.

SEEK OUT THE SELLER'S AGENT

If you want to see a home offered for sale by a real estate company and you intend to ask for a discount, you must seek out the seller's agent.

Just about all agents are paid only commission fees. So if you don't want a buyer's agent, let the agent know that right off. Hand every agent you meet in person your statement of independence. Or, if you are on the phone, make that statement over the phone. Don't leave your independence unstated. An agent might claim the fee and claim to be your agent. In trying to settle that kind of dispute you would be up against the formidable power of the real estate companies. These companies have a long history of cooperation. They stick together. They defend each other. Save yourself.

Also, keep in mind, a seller's agent is most interested in selling the home. You are not a threat to the seller's agent's fee. When you buy a home on your own everyone can win—seller, seller's agent, and you.

> **Q.** What happens if I don't present a Request For Buyer's Agent's Fee Discount to the seller's agent?

> **A.** If you don't state your position immediately and you later buy the home, a seller's agent could claim to also represent you, the buyer. Further, a seller's agent could claim both halves of the commission fee. You could lose any opportunity for negotiating a discount.

KNOCK ON THE SELLER'S DOOR

> **Q.** What can I do if the seller's agent won't return my calls or schedule a time for me to see the home because I'm asking for a discount?

> **A.** Go directly to the seller.

Whenever you have a hard time seeing a home, speak directly to the seller. Expect a seller to welcome you. After all, the seller is waiting for Mr. or Ms. Right Buyer. The seller is eager to sell and interested in showing his or her property to potential buyers.

Explain your predicament to the seller.

- Say you've been unsuccessful in your attempts to see their home through the seller's agent.

- Explain that you are representing yourself.

- Explain that you will ask for a discount of the buyer's agent's fee if you buy the home. Reassure the seller that if you get the discount, the seller does not have to pay any more than already agreed to.

- Point out that your asking for the discount makes the home more salable because it allows you to pay less without costing the seller more.

- Ask to set a time to see the home.

- Leave it to the seller to handle the listing agent. The seller may want to call the agent to be there when you see the home, or may feel the agent isn't doing a good job because you had a hard time seeing the home. Whatever that seller does about the agent is private business between the two of them. You just want to make an appointment to see the home.

Q. May I ask the seller when his or her listing contract with the agent ends, and then, if I want to buy the home, buy it directly from the seller and save all the real estate fees?

A. That depends on the contract between the agent and the seller. But if you are going to wait until the listing contract ends to deal directly with the sellers, *Do not step foot inside the home.* If you cross the threshold when a listing contract is in effect, the owners may have to pay the listing agent the full commission fee. Even if you deal solely with the owners, the small print in the listing contract may allow the listing agent to demand from the owners payment of the

full 6 or 7 percent commission fee, which
then gets passed along to you.

CALCULATE THE DOLLARS YOU DISCOUNT

Each local group of multiple listing companies, by
gentlemen's agreement, sets an agent's full commission
fee for each home listed. This full commission is called
the listing fee. Usually this is 6 or 7 percent of the
price the buyer pays for the home. The multiple listing
office at the board of realtors sets the local split of the
fee between buyer's agent and seller's agent. Usually
the split is close to 50/50. If its different, ask "How
much goes to the buyer's agent?"

> **Q.** Where can I find out our area's listing fee
> and the split between buyer's and seller's
> agent?
>
> **A.** Telephone one of the big real estate com-
> panies in your area and ask two questions.
>
> > 1. How much is your listing fee?
> > 2. What is the split between buyer's
> >   agent and seller's agent?
>
> If the person you talk to says the figures
> are negotiable, ask what they usually are, or
> ask what they were for the last sale made in
> the office. If no one knows the answers, ask
> to speak to the manager.

Let's review. I'll use the same example—with receipts for buyers, sellers, seller's agent, and buyer's
agent—that we started with.

Price Buyer Pays for Home	$80,000
Listing Fee	6%
Agents' Split	50/50
Total Amount of Commission Paid	$4,800
Buyer's Agent's Split of the Fee	$2,400

The formula to find the amount of buyer's agent's fee on any price home is as follows:

- Take the price with the full real estate fee (in the example, $80,000).
- Multiply by the listing fee (in the example, 6 percent).
- Multiply again by the split for the buyer's agent (in the example, .50). That's the discount to ask for.

LEARN BASIC AGENCY WORDS

Agent An individual licensed by the state to engage in the business of helping to bring buyers and sellers together and negotiate prices. An agent must work for a licensed broker.

Board of Realtors A trade association for those who sell homes. Don't let the word "board" impress you as something exclusive. This is not a selected or elected body like the Board of Education or the Board of Directors of a large corporation. The Board of Realtors is more like a union; not just any union, but a union that controls an industry. A member is called a realtor.

Broker A senior-grade agent. Licensed by the state—usually after two years experience as an agent—a broker can form his or her own company, become a partner in a real estate company, or work independently.

Buyer's Agent Presently, this role is without guidelines and open to national debate. The only *true* buyer's agent is one with whom the buyer has a signed contract to act for the buyer and be paid by the buyer. Payment should reward a low price paid for the property by the buyer.

Listing A contract that commits sellers to allow their home to be offered for sale by a real estate company. It obligates the sellers to pay a specified fee—usually 6 or 7 percent of the selling price—when the home is sold. Listing contracts are usually for three or six months.

Listing Agent The person who contracts with the sellers to sell the property and, if successful, collects a fee. Same as seller's agent.

Multiple-Listing A local network of cooperating real estate companies that share their business and split their fees. Usually these companies operate under the umbrella of the local Board of Realtors.

National Association of Realtors A powerful Washington, D.C., lobbying organization known to contribute heavily to lawmakers' election campaigns. This national organization draws its support from local boards of realtors.

Realtor®   A member of the trade association called the Board of Realtors. This membership is usually a prerequuisite for membership in the local multiple listing network.

Single Agency/Exclusive Agency   A recent development in the real estate market whereby agents commit to being loyal to one party in a transaction—either the buyer or the seller. Exclusive agents do not cooperate with the opposing agents, as in multiple listing arrangements, nor do they share business or split fees.

Sub Agent   This is the agent in a multiple listing network who is the salesperson to the buyers and works for the seller in the shadow of the listing agent. Incorrectly, but commonly, called "buyer's agent."

STEP 2

MONEY HUNTING

What you pay to borrow money will likely cost you more than what you pay to buy the home—much more. The interest on $70,000 at 10 percent for a term of 30 years will cost you, over the life of the loan, more than twice the price of the home—$151,148 to be exact. In Step 2 I'll cover points on how you can:

- USE THE TERMS OF THE TRADE

- BE UP FRONT ABOUT THE UP-FRONT COSTS

- GATHER INFORMATION

- WATCH FOR HIDDEN FINANCING COSTS

- QUALIFY FOR A MORTGAGE

- VALUE YOUR STATUS AS A BORROWER

- DOs AND DON'Ts

- LEARN BASIC FINANCING WORDS

It's important to shop for money before you shop for a home because, in addition to the obvious cost of the property you buy, you must also pay to borrow mortgage money to finance the deal. You pay a lender rent for money. Saving on the cost of borrowing money can save you the most on the cost of a home.

Look at these two items as being balanced on opposite ends of a teeter-totter. When you can keep the price you pay the lender "down," you can "up" the price you pay the seller. Consequently, spending "less" for money means you can buy "more" of a home. For example, the ability to make a $614 monthly payment on a 10 percent mortgage means a buyer can borrow $70,000. By comparison, being able to make a $614 monthly payment on a 9 percent mortgage means the buyer can borrow $76,000. Holding down the cost of borrowing money frees up more money to pay for the home.

Keep in mind, too, that most people keep their homes an average of seven to 12 years. In seven years on that same 10 percent mortgage, you will pay more than $47,800 in interest and still owe $66,220 on your $70,000 loan. After 12 years, you will have paid more than $79,920 in interest and still owe $61,460 on that $70,000 loan.

It will be almost 24 years before you will have repaid more than half the principal on your loan. Consider, if you are expecting a child when you accept this $70,000 mortgage, that child will probably be a college graduate before you are halfway through paying off the loan. After 24 years of regular payments, you will still owe more than $33,000.

Q. I can deduct interest on a home loan from my income taxes. Isn't that right?

A. It's right, but confusing. You don't deduct interest paid on a home loan from your taxes directly. You can deduct interest on a home loan from your income. So, if you make $25,000 a year, and you pay interest on a home loan in the amount of $5,000, you report an income of $20,000. Therefore, on the lower income, it follows, your taxes are lower.

USE THE TERMS OF THE TRADE

Take a tip from serious real estate investors. These men and women are as diverse a group of people as ever you'll see, but they speak the language of financing fluently. Learn the meanings and practice using the words in the Basic Financing Words section (pages 41–46) *before* you shop for a mortgage. You'll know more than most buyers and sellers, and more than most people who work for mortgage lenders.

> **Q.** What makes a mortgage different from other loans?
>
> **A.** A mortgage is a loan made specifically to an owner of real estate, which gives the lender a claim to the property until the loan is paid. There are laws and laws and laws to safeguard homeowners. And there are strict legal procedures for lenders to follow. The laws on mortgages vary locally, so check for exact information with a lawyer, escrow or title agent, or the city or county attorney.

What befuddles many buyers is the mortgage jargon—the use of abbreviations, slang terms, and initials. It's confusing to the uninitiated. Using the correct terms is vital to saving money. There's probably no investment of a few hours of time that will save you more money than learning to speak the language of financing.

BE UP FRONT ABOUT UP-FRONT COSTS

Interest is not the entire cost of a mortgage. Interest is the star of the show. Interest gets the publicity. Every move it makes—up or down—is reported on the evening news and newspaper front pages.

Neglected are the up-front costs. "What costs?" asks anyone whose experience with mortgages does not extend into the 1980s. Along with banking deregulation came the up-front costs. They are strange to most buyers, are rarely questioned or compared, and can add up to a staggering amount.

> **Q.** I sense something twisted here. Are the up-front costs additional to interest charges? Must I have money before I can borrow money?
>
> **A.** Exactly. You must pay to borrow money. Often buyers don't have enough for a down payment and up-front costs. That's why sellers often agree to pay some or all of the up-front costs for buyers to get a mortgage.

Buyers and sellers can go round and round about who will pay the up-front costs. Problems most often arise when the costs are unexpected. Knowing that there will be up-front costs, and how you would like to deal with them, will solve the problems before they arise. The following example shows what I mean.

Doug and the seller have just agreed on a price for a home at $80,000. It's going to cost $4,000 in up-front costs to get the mortgage he needs.

Doug plans to pay the cost himself, so there's no problem. He is prepared to pay the $4,000 plus the price of the home. He looks upon the price of the home as a total of $84,000.

But if Doug expected the sellers to pay any up-front costs out of the $80,000 agreed to, he'd be in trouble. For the seller to pay any up-front costs would mean, in effect, selling their home for less than the agreed price.

Being up front about the up-front costs is the surest way to prevent any misunderstanding. If, in this example, Doug wanted the seller to pay the up-front costs, he would have a sales contract with the seller for $84,000—with seller paying the up-front costs.

The point is this: If you don't have enough money to pay the down payment the mortgage requires and the up-front costs, be up front about it with the seller from the beginning. Sellers are usually agreeable to paying these costs when the price they agree to accept reflects the addition of the up-front costs.

Q. What are the up-front costs of a mortgage?

A. They are any charges that the lender charges before the lender will lend you money. They can be labeled points or lender's fee, credit check or appraisal fee, even mortgage brokerage fee. Mortgage insurance can be paid up front or added to your monthly payment. Know the basic financing words and what they mean. Use the terms. If a lender says something you don't understand, ask questions.

GATHER INFORMATION

To get an idea of the current mortgage market, start with a conventional mortgage from your local bank or savings and loan association. This will be the yardstick against which you'll measure other types of financing.

Check out the Federal Housing Administration (FHA) and the Veterans Administration (VA) if you are entitled. Spend an hour on the phone with the yellow pages on your lap opened to *Mortgages*. Call the big lenders whose names you recognize. Call the small lenders. Call at least four or five to get started. Ask each of them their current costs and write these on the Financing Comparison Worksheet (page 47).

On weekends, or whenever your newspaper has a shelter or home section, check for lender advertisements. Call them and ask for a rundown of the information on the worksheet.

When you have a loan officer on the phone, ask if they mail out flyers with changes in mortgage rates. If they do, ask to be on their mailing list. Ask them to mail you all the information and brochures they have on mortgages, and if they have a telephone hotline for mortgage rate updates. Keep the hotline numbers handy.

Mortgage rates change frequently. Points change often, too, sometimes overnight. And just one point less on a $70,000 mortgage can save you $700 cash up front. Prepare to check the rates at least every week or 10 days when you are shopping for a home. Stay on top of the mortgage picture; when you find a home, you'll be ready.

After you sign a sales contract, call a mortgage hotline daily. Between the time you apply for a loan and the actual closing will be the date when you must "lock in" the points and interest rate at which you will accept the loan. One buyer said that by calling a hotline daily—and by locking in the points when they were lowest—he saved $1,500.

Q. Does financing affect the price?

A. Definitely. Buyers will pay more for a home where the mortgage interest rate is lower than the going interest rate. This can happen when there is an assumable mortgage or a private mortgage provided by the sellers. Paying less for the money, the buyers are usually willing to pay more for the home.

WATCH FOR HIDDEN FINANCING COSTS

Not only do real estate companies cooperate with each other and not compete for fees, but with banking deregulation, they also offer mortgages. It is up to the buyer to compare the mortgage offered with what is available elsewhere.

Q. Isn't it a great convenience to get a loan at a real estate company?

A. Yes, but what does it cost? Buying a home and picking up a mortgage on your way out does not carry the same price tag as stopping for a loaf of bread and picking up a quart of milk at the 7-11. The cost you pay for a mortgage makes comparing several—at least 10—worthwhile.

Examine the cost of convenience at the one-stop real estate office and loan maker. The cost of a mortgage, wherever you get it, has to give you the best value for what you need. Convenience may be worth the cost to you. All I say is, know the cost before you sign for the loan.

Q. I understand that the airline and banking industries were deregulated at about the same time. Why then is it uncommon to hear of cost cutting in mortgages like those that have come to be expected in airline fares?

A. I don't know the answer, but I can tell you what I see—or rather what I don't see. I don't see people comparison-shopping for mortgages like they do air fares. People seem to accept the terms of a mortgage without shopping around.

When shopping for a mortgage, suspect lower-than-current interest rates.

Mortgages with low—startlingly low—interest rates and no up-front costs can be the cheese in the mouse-trap. Watch out. Look around. A low-cost mortgage is sometimes offered by home builders or developers. And the low cost may be well suited to your needs.

But beware. The cost of the money is in the price of the home. Ask, "How much am I paying for the financing?" You might have trouble getting a straight answer. The financing may have been arranged in a big package including many homes or many projects.

You might have only the price of the property to compare. If the mortgage interest rate is very low, is the price of the home very high? Would it be hard to resell? Is the home overpriced compared to similar properties? You can be sure that if you are not writing a check to the lender for the mortgage, you are paying for the mortgage in the price.

Before you buy, determine how much extra you are paying. Is the home worth that price to you? *Awareness* makes the difference. How much are you paying for the home? How much for the financing? If no one will tell you, your worksheet on mortgages can help. You can see what mortgages cost. What would it cost in points, origination fee, mortgage insurance, etc., to get a mortgage like the one offered here?

QUALIFY FOR A MORTGAGE

How a lender looks at you as a candidate for a loan depends on the following:

- Your credit history.

- Your job and income.

- Your present investments; other real estate, securities.

- Your present long-term debts—long-term generally means with more than six months of payments still due.

- Your cash available to put toward the price of the home. Understandably, lenders feel more comfortable risking their loan money to you when they know that you risk yours, too.

Q. How do I find out how much I can borrow?

A. You can get a pretty good idea by meeting with a mortgage loan officer at your local savings and loan. But a firm commitment from a lender will have to wait until you have a sales contract to buy a particular home because the home you buy and the price you pay is factored into their decision to lend you money.

I highly recommend that buyers, especially first-time buyers, find out from a lender how much they can qualify to borrow before looking at homes. Make an appointment with a loan officer. He or she will have the formulas used to determine your borrowing power—the amount you can pay back based on the amount you earn.

My first choice for a loan officer would be at the banking institution where you have your savings and checking accounts. My second choice would be a place where you think you'd like to do business. Either place will love an opportunity to show you what a good program they have in hopes of getting your business once you decide on a home.

Bring to the appointment all the figures you will need, such as your gross monthly income and your federal, state, and social security taxes withheld from your gross income. Also bring along a list of your long-term debts: car payments, child support, student loans, and any other loans on which you'll be making payments for more than six months. And calculate a specific amount of cash you can pay toward a home. If you can pay 20 percent down, you may not have to pay for costly mortgage insurance. Keep in mind that the more cash you can put in, the less costly your loan will be; and the less costly the loan, the more home you can get with the least money.

VALUE YOUR STATUS AS A BORROWER

The business of mortgage lending is not only vast and intimidating, but also enormously competitive. However, you, the borrower, are eyed approvingly.

In fact, the total amount of debt we Americans incur for buying homes is second only to the debt the United States incurs to run the government.

So take advantage of the behind-the-scenes clamoring for your favors. Do not go mortgage begging with hat in hand. Shop for the financing as carefully as you shop for the home. Remember, you'll pay more for the money than you pay for the home. And what you pay for the money has no resale value—poof, it's gone.

Look at yourself and see how good you look to a lender.

The rate of interest a lender gets from a mortgage is generally 3–4 percent higher than what the lender could get from a savings account or money market fund.

Money is most safe in your hands. Defaults and foreclosures are rare; devastating, but rare. Mostly, mortgage borrowers have a model record. The check you write for the roof over your head gets into the mail each month even when it means skimping on groceries.

For the lender, mortgages are secure and flexible. Mortgages can be bought, sold, and traded between lenders. Mortgages can be gathered into a pile and sold to investors. If you want to invest in mortgages, you can buy shares of stock in Fannie Mae on the New York Stock Market. For you, the mortgage stays on the home. But for the investor, that note you sign is movable and salable.

Mortgages have long been a safe haven for squirreling away money. As a result, money comes from university funds, pension funds, foreign investors, and big charitable foundations. Homeowners can be trusted to keep that money safe and profitable for the various lenders.

So, find the lender who will charge you least, in the least threatening manner. Remember, the lender needs you as much as you need the loan. Give the favor of your borrowing only when you get the lowest cost.

DOs AND DON'Ts

DO know that when it comes to borrowing money there is no free lunch. When a home is offered for sale with financing included in the price, be aware that you are paying for that financing. Ask, "How much for the home? How much for the financing?"

DON'T be lured into buying a home with low-interest financing without being aware of the up-front costs buried in the price.

DO be independent, speak the mortgage language, compare costs of competitive lenders, know what's going on and exactly what you are paying for the money.

DON'T forget when it comes to borrowers, you're second in prestige only to Uncle Sam.

DO shop the mortgage market by phone and in advertisements—look for sales. All dollars are good. Rent them at the lowest interest rate and with the least expensive up-front costs.

DON'T think you have to take the first mortgage lender that comes along.

DO expect answers to all your questions.

DON'T accept a mortgage blindly.

LEARN BASIC FINANCING WORDS

Amortization Table A schedule for repaying a loan. Usually the same payment is made each month. The amount of payment includes interest owed for the previous month plus some of the principal. When the term of the mortgage ends, and all payments have been made, the loan is paid in full. For example, for each $1,000 borrowed at 10 percent interest for 30 years:

Date	Payment	Interest	Principal	Balance on Loan
1st Month	$8.78	$8.33	$0.45	$999.55
2nd Month	$8.78	$8.33	$0.45	$999.10

(To calculate the next month's figures, use this formula: Multiply the Balance on Loan by the 10 percent interest rate, then divide by 12; that gives you the month's interest you owe. Deduct the Interest for that month from the Payment to calculate the amount paid toward the Principal. Deduct the Principal payment from the previous month's Balance on Loan for the new Balance on Loan.)

3rd Month	$8.78	$8.33	$0.45	$998.65

Appraisal An estimate of the value of property. Always, no matter how an appraiser tries to be impartial, the estimate is colored by the appraiser's own point of view.

Balloon Payment A chunk of principal due on a loan at a specified time. The payment could be due during the life of the mortgage or at the end of the mortgage term. A mortgage could read either of the following ways on the promissory note: "On November 1, 1990, $10,000 principal payment due" (in such a case the monthly payments march along as scheduled), or "On November 1, 1990, all monies owed for interest and principal are due and payable."

Closing Costs Expenses payable before title of a property is transferred. Negotiable between buyer and seller as to who pays. Included are fees for: escrow; recording the deed; title insurance; appraisal and inspection; abstracting; and real estate commission.

Contract for Deed or Land Contract A method by which sellers allow buyers time to pay for the property. Sellers finance the purchase and keep the deed until the amount stated in the contract is paid.

Credit Report Verification of borrower's ability to repay money requested and past payment record.

Down Payment The amount of cash that buyers pay toward the price of a property. Included is earnest money paid at the signing of the sales contract. Not included is money paid for points or other up-front fees charged by the lender for issuing the mortgage.

Due on Sale A requirement in the small print of some mortgage contracts stating that if the property is sold, the loan must be paid in full. It keeps new owners from assuming the old mortgage.

Earnest Money A monetary deposit—made with a lawyer or escrow or title agent when sales contract is signed—given as evidence of a buyer's sincerity to buy.

Equity The value of property less what is owed. In other words, the seller's stake in the property; what the sellers expect to get out of it. If a property sells for $60,000 and the sellers have $40,000 in mortgage and other claims owed, their equity is $20,000.

Escrow Holding by a neutral third party of funds and/or documents

Interest Money paid for use of money. The rate is stated as an annual percentage of the principal owed.

Fixed Rate The interest charged on a mortgage stays the same for the life of the loan.

Adjustable Rate The interest rate that is charged on a mortgage fluctuates. It usually goes up or down depending on the interest rate paid on government-secured loans of like term. For instance, rates that are adjustable annually are tied to one-year securities rates. The rates of adjustable mortgages are normally two or three percentage points higher than the securities' rates.

Land Contract or Contract for Deed A method by which sellers allow buyers time to pay for the property. Sellers, in effect, finance the purchase. Buyers take possession. Sellers keep the deed until the amount stated in the contract is paid.

Lock In This happens after applying for a mortgage. Locking in reserves the actual dollars—at a specific interest rate and with fixed up-front costs—which a mortgage company will lend you. Your lender will have a policy as to how long before your scheduled closing date you must "set" the interest rate and points.

Monthly Payments The amount set in the mortgage agreement. Usually covers the interest owed for the previous month and part of the principal.

Mortgage A loan that applies to real estate. Borrowers sign a promissory note to repay the amount borrowed and give lender a right to take possession of the property if the borrowers default. Local laws exist to protect the rights of borrowers and lenders.

> **Assumable Mortgage** New owners can take over the former owners' obligation and continue the prescribed payments. Sellers do not have to pay off the mortgage when property is sold.

> **Conventional Mortgage** A mortgage loan not insured by the F.H.A. or guaranteed by the V.A.

FHA Mortgage A Federal Housing Administration loan made by a private lender to a private borrower and insured by the F.H.A. Since the F.H.A. insures the loan, it sets standards on the condition of the home and standards on the financial condition of the borrower. Many first-time borrowers use F.H.A. financing because of the low down-payment requirement.

First Mortgage The claim at the head of the line to take possession of the property over other claims, should the borrowers default.

VA Mortgage A Veterans Administration loan is available to eligible armed service veterans. The loans are long-term and allow for low down payments. The loans are made by private lenders to private, eligible borrowers. The Veterans Administration protects the lenders against loss.

Second Mortgage Second in line to claim possession of the property in case of default.

Mortgage Insurance A policy where borrowers pay premiums to assure benefits are paid to the lender to pay off the mortgage in case of death or default. Frequently required by lenders when borrowers have paid less than a 20 percent down payment.

Origination Fee The fee charged by lenders to prepare loan documents.

P.I.T.I. The costs often included in a monthly payment. Stands for Principal, Interest, Taxes, and Insurance.

Points Sometimes called "interest paid in advance." Points lower the interest rate. (1 point equals 1 percent of the loan; 1 point on an $80,000 mortgage is $800.) A mortgage with an interest rate of 10 percent and 0 points might be secured at 9.5 percent and 2 points or 9 percent and 4 points. Experts generally recommend, since paying points is pre-payment of interest, keeping points at a minimum. Points change—sometimes daily. As buyers prepare to finalize a mortgage agreement, they should pay close attention to these changes.

Price The cash down payment plus the money borrowed that it takes to buy a home. (Buyers may have additional costs in acquiring real estate property such as legal advice, cost of points, and origination fee for financing.)

Principal The lump sum of money owed. Interest is calculated as a percentage of principal still owed.

Promissory Note A pledge to pay an amount borrowed. With a mortgage, the lender can claim a right to the property if borrowers fail to make payments as promised.

Purchase Money Mortgage Sellers hold the mortgage on the property. Sellers take a mortgage so that buyers can purchase the property.

Seller Financing Similar to Purchase Money Financing except that it does not always constitute a legal mortgage. Since the seller is a one-time lender to a one-time buyer, the manner of securing the loan may be some arrangement other than what is specifically called a mortgage; it could be any manner agreed upon by the buyer and the seller. It can be a land contract, a contract for deed, or a trust deed arrangement. But whatever it is, the buyer and the seller should have the documents prepared by legal advisers.

Term of the Mortgage The time before a mortgage contract ends.

Terms of the Mortgage Conditions under which a mortgage is given, such as 10 percent interest rate, for 30 years.

Trust Deed A manner of mortgaging a property involving three parties: the lender, the borrower, and a trustee. The lender comes up with the money; the borrower gives a promissory note and deeds the property to the lender for security in getting repayment of the money; and the trustee holds title to the property until one of two things happens: 1) The note is paid and the title is passed to the borrower or 2) the note is not paid and the lender, exercising the right given in the trust deed, asks trustee to sell the property and pay the lender what is owed.

FINANCING COMPARISON WORKSHEET

For a Loan in the Amount of $ __50,000__

Lender	Mort. Inc.	Solid Bank	City Sand L	
Up-Front Costs				
Lender's Fees	3%	2%	2%	
Points	1.5	1.5	2.75	
Mortgage Insurance	No	No	No	
Other				
Interest Rate %				
Fixed Rate	9.75%		9.8%	
Adjustable Rate		7.875%		
Years of Loan	15	30	30	
Down Payment Required	$10,000	$10,000	$10,000	
Monthly Payment				
Principal & Interest Only	$529.68	$362.52	$435.10	
Principal, Interest, Taxes, & Insurance				

STEP 3

FINDING OUT WHAT'S REALLY FOR SALE

Traditionally, in the home market, buying is passive, selling is aggressive. Step 3 will turn that around for you and suggest that you:

- GET AGGRESSIVE

- PLAY THE ADVERTISING GAME

- REACH OWNERS IN A SECURE BUILDING

- TOUCH THE SLEEPING SELLERS

- UTILIZE THE MULTIPLE-LISTING SYSTEM

- FIND OUT-OF-TOWN PROPERTY

- STRETCH YOUR IMAGINATION

I once heard a man refer to a woman real estate agent as a "pushy broad." Talk about typecasting! But in a crude way the example helps me make a point: Even in a so-called buyers market, home buyers tend to lie down and get walked on.

> **Q.** Why is it that all the "push" goes for sellers?
>
> **A.** Sellers pay the commission fee. Buyers pay it in the end, of course. But money goes from the seller's hand to agents hand. It's that old Chinese proverb: Favors flow naturally toward the source of money.

Put on your stomping shoes, wear your power suit. Attack the shell of secrecy that surrounds homes for sale. If you plan to buy independently to get the best home for the best price, you'll need to push. You've got to uncover a wide range of homes not obviously "for sale." You've got to meet sellers eyeball to eyeball, one on one. Here's how.

GET AGGRESSIVE

Share with friends.

Tell everyone you know that you are looking to buy a home directly from the owners. Do you worry you'll get trapped in a situation where you'll be afraid of hurting a friend's feelings? It's good you feel that way. Don't lose that refreshing sensitivity. But practice saying, "Sorry, that's not it. I have something in mind. I'll know it when I see it. Thanks for bringing it to my attention. If you hear of anything else, please let me know."

And keep it going. When you see someone in the grocery who lives where you are interested in living ask them, "Have you heard of any of your neighbors who are interested in selling their homes?"

Buying on tips from friends and family is the way a great many homes are sold. Don't neglect using this resource for finding a home. Enlist everyone's help— your car pool, bridge club, Bible study group, the gang at work, the exercise club.

See inside every home you can.

Do the obvious things people do when looking for homes. Answer classified ads. Pop in where you see "Open House" signs out front. (Don't forget your Request for Buyer's Agent's Fee Discount in case you run into a multiple listing agent.) Even see inside homes you know are out of the neighborhood or the price range you have targeted in order to become the most well-informed buyer possible. Add what you see to your information bank. Look upon each home you find as more research in your independent study of buying a home.

(In Step 4, I suggest things to look for once you're inside a home and how to judge whether a particular home is what you are looking for. But, for now, I'll stick to finding out what's for sale. Unfortunately, not all homes for sale have signs out front and are advertised in the Sunday newspapers.)

PLAY THE ADVERTISING GAME

Place an ad in the "Homes For Sale" classified sections of community newspapers. The same "For Sale" section where you look to find homes to buy.

> **Q.** Why do you say place a "Wanted to Buy" ad in the "For Sale" section?
>
> **A.** Because while buyers check that section for what is selling, so do sellers.

Keep the price of the ad down. Some advertising people believe running a small ad can be as, or more, effective than a big ad. In any case, make every word count and place the ad frequently.

Try a simple ad with minimal words, all capital letters, single-spacing, and centered lines. An example:

```
WANTED TO BUY:
DIRECT FROM OWNERS
2-BD, 2-BATH CONDO
H: 176-6767 W: 177-1897
```

Give your home and work telephone numbers. It makes reaching you easy and that's important. Some callers won't persist if they can't reach you the first time. These calls are the reason for your ad. Since they are what you pay for, arrange to get every one. If you can't answer the phone have someone do it who can get information from a caller. At least get their name and phone number so that you can call them back.

Personally, I like a phone answered by a machine when the party isn't available. It saves time. You get your message in and you don't have to keep trying to reach them. They'll get your message.

Q. What if we don't get any calls?

A. Make sure you've run the ad a few times. Repetition is important. Then, if there is still no response, cancel the ad. Try another paper or periodical—a local paper, a throwaway, maybe a newsletter you get from work or a church or club you belong to.

Post an index card on bulletin boards.

Wording for an index card can be the same as the classified ad above with the addition of your name and address. It won't cost more to add the personal touch of who you are. And it will make your notice stand out to someone who knows you or knew your sister in high school.

Bulletin boards are not just message exchanges. Some, as in a condo building I know, are little gossip centers attracting residents.

Q. Where can I find bulletin boards?

A. When you start looking you'll be amazed at how many are out there. Some likely places are shopping centers—look especially near where you want to live—exercise clubs, town house projects, office complexes, grocery stores.

Printing and distributing a flyer is a good way to do a fine sweep of a territory. Describe what you would like to find and blanket the area where you'd like to live.

Too aggressive for you? Remember, you have to be aggressive, meet the sellers eyeball to eyeball. A flyer distributed in the neighborhood is an effective way to sell a home. If it can be done to sell a home, the more reason to do it to buy a home.

Q. What would it cost to make up a flyer?

A. For $20 you can reach a lot of potential sellers. A cut-rate photo copy shop will duplicate 200 copies for less than $10. For another $10 you could get a couple of moonlighting paper boys to take your message door to door on a Saturday morning.

Or, better yet, take it around yourself. It could be fun. You'd get to meet and chat with people and find out if you'd really like to live there.

The flyer could read something like this:

WANTED TO BUY
A HOUSE IN THE LAKES AREA

WE ARE INDEPENDENT BUYERS LOOKING FOR A HOME TO BUY DIRECTLY FROM THE OWNERS.

OUR FIRST CHOICE IS A HOUSE OF VICTORIAN VINTAGE THAT HAS BEEN WELL MAINTAINED AND IS IN GOOD CONDITION. OK IF IT NEEDS A LITTLE PAINT AND POLISH, BUT NOTHING MAJOR LIKE WIRING AND STRUCTURAL WORK.

WE WILL CONSIDER OTHER STYLES OF HOUSES, BUT THEY MUST HAVE AT LEAST ONE FIREPLACE AND TWO BATHROOMS. WE WOULD LIKE A YARD WITH SPACE FOR A GARDEN.

NEW FINANCING IS NO PROBLEM. WE ARE A PROFESSIONAL COUPLE. HOWEVER, WE PREFER AN ASSUMABLE MORTGAGE OR SELLER FINANCING.

TRISH AND RON HUGHES
HOME: 555-9080
RON'S WORK: 555-7968 TRISH'S WORK: 555-5678

REACH OWNERS IN A SECURE BUILDING

Reaching owners in a secure condominium building may take a little extra effort. However, it could be well worth it. The condo market has been slow and there are many owners wishing they could sell who are not actively in the market. There are some good buys available.

To find them, ask the caretaker if you can leave a flyer for each resident. Or, if that's not workable, ask to leave a stack near where people pick up their mail. But either way, you'll only reach people who live in the building and not the owners renting their places. Better yet, ask the association manager for a list of the owners. Explain that you want to contact them because you're looking for a place to buy. If the manager can't give you the names of all the owners, ask how you can reach them. Will the manager forward the flyer?

Assure the association manager that the owners would like to hear from a potential buyer. The manager would be doing the owners a disservice not to help you reach them.

Another effective way to reach these people will take a little time. Mail a postcard to each condo addressed to its owner; "Owner Unit #101," "Owner #102," etc. The caretaker should at least give you the unit numbers. Next to the address write: Please Forward. The post office might have a forwarding address for the owner who has moved. The renter may also have the address. On the message side of the postcard simply state:

> WANTED TO BUY:
> A CONDO IN FAIRMONT BUILDING
> DIRECTLY FROM THE OWNER. PREFER 2 BEDROOM, 2 BATH, WITH VIEW OF THE WOODS. However, we are flexible. We prefer a price in the $90,000 range with seller financing.
> Cecily and Bryan.
> Phone: (H) 555-5678
> (W)-His: 555-7654 (W)-Hers: 555-7659

Q. Who will I reach with a flyer that I won't reach following the ads?

A. I call them sleepers. They are people who want to sell. They're ready, but not actively doing anything about it just now except following how the sales in their area are going and keeping tabs on what's selling.

TOUCH THE SLEEPING SELLERS

Some of these sleeping sellers I have in mind are similar to the following:

Mr. and Mrs. Kelly listed their home for sale with an agent. The home didn't sell, the listing expired. They are deciding what to do next. Should they list again with the same agent? Try someone else? Or try selling it themselves? Meanwhile, they're taking a breather while they decide.

Mr. Jones rented his home when he couldn't sell it. The home hadn't sold and he had to move to take a job in another town. He's counting on the rent coming in to pay the home's expenses, but he still wants to sell it. He prays for buyers to come along, but wants minimum disturbance to the renters.

Mrs. Johnson is planning to sell in the near future. She's made up her mind. She's just waiting for the end of winter and her daughter's wedding.

Mr. and Mrs. Egan need to sell but dread it. They just can't seem to get themselves up for strangers coming through their home. They hate to think of racing around before work making beds, doing dishes, disrupting their routine. Just the thought that someone will critically eye their home terrifies them because they had a bad experience selling their first home. Plus, they've lived there so long, pulling up roots is hard.

Dr. Dean has property listed with a real estate agent. It's an open listing allowing him to sell it himself and not pay a fee if he does. He's not happy with the way things are going, the service he's getting, the advertising, or the time it's taking. He's going to ask to cancel the listing. He has decided to look for buyers himself.

UTILIZE THE MULTIPLE-LISTING SYSTEM

Q. We live in an area where a great many homes are sold through the multiple listing network. But we don't know which homes are for sale unless there is a sign or an ad. Is there a way we can find other homes in the multiple listing network that are for sale?

A. Agents differ on how freely they allow buyers to peek into the multiple listing catalog of homes for sale. You'll have to ask individual agents.

Some will protect the catalog like a secret weapon. Claiming protection of seller's privacy, these agents will want to choose for you which homes they think suit you.

I am of the opposite point of view. The information in the catalog is not personal and in need of protection. It's factual. I've often argued with other agents that sellers who list their homes with agents should have the widest possible exposure to buyers. Regularly, I'd give the catalog to buyers to take home overnight. Both buyers and sellers, I feel strongly, should have free and open access to the information.

Some agents would have fits when I'd say the catalogs should be on the shelf of the reference department of the local public

library. You can't know for sure how an
agent will respond to your request. Ask.

FIND OUT-OF-TOWN PROPERTY

When you are looking for a place in an area where you
are not currently living, finding property is no problem. In this situation, too, you can use the mail and
advertising techniques discussed earlier.

Set a date, say in 30 days, when you will be in
your new area. Aim for appointments to see homes
when you arrive.

Also, subscribe to the local newspapers for as short
a term as possible. Newspapers usually have a policy
regarding minimum subscription time. It can be one
month, three months, or one year. To mail you the
copies, they'll want the payment in advance.

Place a Wanted to Buy ad something like this:

```
OUT OF TOWN BUYER
Wants 3-Bedroom home
near bus line. 312-555-3489
```

Contact owners and agents who have advertised
homes for sale in the newspaper. Telephone—or write
if there is time—for appointments to see the property.
Remember to request the buyer's agent's fee discount
from all agents.

Make up a flyer and, along with a Buyer's Agent's
Fee Discount Statement, mail a copy to every real estate company in the yellow pages.

If you are going to work for an established business in the new area, mail a flyer to the personnel office. Ask them to post it on the employee bulletin
board.

STRETCH YOUR IMAGINATION

As you begin to find out what's for sale, stretch your imagination; my grandmother raised a family in the back of a grocery store. Today, for the inventive buyer, there is a wide range of opportunities—duplexes, apartment buildings, fix-up specials, new developments. On the following Home Options form, list the possibilities and weigh their costs.

HOME OPTIONS FORM

Possibilities	Cost Consequence
7530 Sangamon 30 Yrs. Old Rambler	$90,000 Price — Plus Cost of Renovating — ($10,000 ?)
4700 Lakeshore Condominium	$110,000 Price — Assoc. Expenses $150/Mo. — Subject to change??
7900 Sogar St. Duplex	$120,000 Price — Rental Income $450/Mo. Tax Advantages ???

SHOPPING SMART

Real estate companies make millions of dollars primarily because buyers and sellers can't get close to each other. With a little planning, consideration, communication, and thought, you can become a diplomatic buyer who can work closely with sellers to make the best deal for everyone involved. In Step 4 you will:

- USE GOOD HOME-BUYING MANNERS
- EXPECT TO "FALL IN LOVE"
- PICTURE LIVING THERE
- DECIDE HOW THE HOME FITS YOUR LIFE-STYLE
- EXPLORE THE NEIGHBORHOOD
- WRITE DOWN VITAL STATISTICS

You ring the doorbell at the appointed time. You are standing on the front step of a home for sale advertised by the sellers in Sunday's classified ads. When the door opens, the person you meet may be someone you later meet again over the bargaining table.

Remember that. Remember also that often the reason buyers don't buy directly from sellers is they don't get along. Buyers and sellers can work together. Smarten up and you can save 6 or 7 percent of the price you pay. On a $100,000 home thats $6,000 or $7,000 lopped off the price. Its up to you, the buyer, to take the initiative to make it work.

> **Q.** You said in Step 3, Finding a Home, to be aggressive. Now are you saying, "cool it"?
>
> **A.** No, not really. You, the buyer, must be aggressive. You have to look out for yourself. You have to see everything, ask questions as they come to mind. Doing it courteously and diplomatically, however, pays dividends.

USE GOOD HOME-BUYING MANNERS

When calling in response to an advertisement, identify yourself. Tell the seller, "I'm calling about your home for sale. My name is Bryan. We saw your ad in the paper. We are looking for a home in your neighborhood that we can buy directly from the owners. Could I make an appointment to see your place?"

In the beginning, see all properties. You're laying the groundwork for the price you'll offer when you find the home you want. You'll get a feel for prices—it's not a science. That this 4-bedroom rambler is a bargain at $97,000 and that one at $97,000 is overpriced, you will learn from experience.

Q. We only want a home with a family room. Shouldn't we ask before we bother to see a property, "Does it have a family room?"

A. No, see all properties. See for yourself what the home has to offer for the price being asked. And you may be crazy enough about a home with no family room that you would convert a bedroom or build on the space you want.

Ask only for the appointment. Speak slowly, distinctly, spell out your name so the listener can write it down. Give your phone number at work and at home. The owner, checking on you, can call you back.

If a machine answers, always leave your name and number. Do this even if you won't be available to receive a return call. Say, "Here's my number, but we'll be away for the weekend. I'll call you again on Monday." Sellers will appreciate your consideration.

When you visit a home for sale, if you have a business card, hand it to the person who opens the door. Introduce yourself. "I'm Doug. I have an appointment to see your home at three o'clock."

Q. What if no adult is home and a child answers and says that his mother said that it was OK for us to come in and look around?

A. Don't enter. Ask when an adult will be home. Call then and make another appointment.

Once inside the home, keep in mind that you are looking at someone's nest. Be gentle. To you, the buyers, the home is a commodity—bricks, mortar, squared-off rooms. To the owners, the home is permanently woven into their lives.

That home could be giving the owner big emotional tugs and you can't possibly know what's going on. The tugs could be happy memories—a new baby brought home, wedding gifts piled on the dining room table, a busy kitchen with Thanksgiving turkey. Or maybe you have intruded on sad memories—sickness, betrayal, divorce, a lot of pain.

> **Q.** Am I weird? I'm uncomfortable in a private home walking around and looking closely at what I want to see. The seller watching me makes it worse.
>
> **A.** No, you're considerate of others. It's good that you don't feel free to poke around like you're in Sears. But be open about asking questions and seeing what you need to. Ask to open cupboards and look in every room. Sellers expect it. They want to sell.

The upshot of this good-manners lesson is this: Sellers are known to negotiate differently with different buyers. The most desperate-to-sell sellers have been heard to say about rude buyers, "I wouldn't sell to those so-and-sos if they paid in solid gold." And another time, when three buyers were competing, bidding up the price of a home, the sellers said, "We want that nice couple to get it. We'll take the price they offer."

EXPECT TO "FALL IN LOVE"

One other touch—expect something "special."

The quality of this feeling is referred to in different ways. One real estate tycoon I know says he buys a building "that speaks to me." A classy woman I sold a home to said she was looking for a home "that chooses me." Whatever you call it, you can't always put your finger on it, but you'll feel it.

It's important. Look for a home that, as I say, you fall in love with. That's not too much to expect. In fact, considering the high prices of homes today, it makes sense. Whatever you pay, it's too much unless that home has the extra something special that speaks to you, chooses you, or makes you fall in love.

PICTURE LIVING THERE

When you view a home, mentally move in your household. Rate the home 1 to 10 on the following checklist and call in experts for estimates as you need to.

- How would your furniture fit?
- How much renovation or repair is required?
- What would it cost to make any necessary changes?
- What is the present condition of the home?
  - Decorating: paint, carpet, flooring, tile?
  - Mechanical: heating, air conditioning, electrical?
  - Structural: foundation, walls, plaster, floors, roof?
  - Kitchen: cupboards, counters, appliances (which are included)?
  - Bathrooms: shower, fixtures, water pressure?

DECIDE HOW THE HOME FITS YOUR LIFE-STYLE

- *The flow of rooms:* How would morning traffic move from bedroom to bath to kitchen? Could one person go to bed early or sleep in in the morning without being disturbed?

- *Privacy:* Some families live by the rule that every person needs a spot where they can be alone. Is there a spot for everyone?

- *Gathering place:* Is there a spot to fit the immediate family? The extended family? This could be the kitchen table, dining room, fireplace seating area, barbecue area, or around a television set or hot tub.

- *Overnight guests:* Is there space or does the house provide an excuse to plead, "Sorry, no room at the inn"?

Think, too, about the property and landscape that surround the home.

- Do you see green in summer out the window? Is it important?

- Is there a nighttime view of lights? Do you like that?

- Is there room for a garden, deck, patio, fence, pool, tennis court, or a play yard for children?

- Can you see the sunset or the sunrise?

People differ strongly about the sun; love it or hate it. I sold a home that buyers bought specifically because they loved the rooms flooded with sunshine during the morning hours. The sellers sold the home specifically because of the same flooding sunshine. They hated it. If you have strong opinions, check the home at various times of day.

EXPLORE THE NEIGHBORHOOD

Does the street look like a place you'd be happy to come home to? One home buyer I know chose the

homes he liked by the look of the street and the outside of the home. He never got out of the car. Later,
his wife looked at the insides of the homes he had cho-
sen from the outside. She chose one and, of course,
they both liked it.

Does the neighborhood offer what is most important to you?

- Convenience to work, schools, night school,
  university, clubs, exercise, sports, theaters, res-
  taurants, shopping, marketing?

- People close by—family, singles, retirees, a ra-
  cial and age mixture, working people, house-
  wives at home, party givers, library quiet,
  renters, owners?

- Transportation nearby—car pool, buses, free-
  ways, train, airport?

WRITE DOWN THE VITAL STATISTICS

Comparing homes will be easier with a tool that helps
you standardize your measurements.

For each home you view have a copy of the Vital
Statistics Form shown on page 69. Fill in the blanks,
asking the sellers for what you need if they don't provide it. You'll make better decisions on what to buy
and when to negotiate prices with critical information
about the homes logically arrayed before you.

On the information sheets, differences in homes
show up, such as:

- *Costs.* Price is only one of the costs. What are
  financing costs, property taxes, utilities, any association or management fees, and insurance
  costs?

- *What you don't remember.* Say you're a kitchen
  person. You spent time in one home checking
  out kitchen cupboards, counter space, and ap-

pliances. Later, you can't remember: Did that home have three or four bedrooms?

- *Points you may have missed.* It was a cloudy day when you visited that home and the decorating was awful and depressing. You didn't stay long. Later, on paper, you see the size of the living room is just what you like and it has a fireplace. Redecorating may make a difference. It's worth a call to see again.

Q. What should we look for in comparing vital statistics on homes for sale?

A. A home you love at a price you love. That's what this process of buying independently is all about.

VITAL STATISTICS FORM

Asking Price $79,000   Date 1·7·90
Address 123 Main Street
Seller's Name Erickson, Peg and Mac
Home Phone 439· 8721   Work Phone

Financing Offered: Assumable Mortgage (X) Seller Mortgage ( )
Other ( ) Terms: 8% — $40,000
Present Mortgage Lender: 1ST National

Current Expenses: Property Taxes for 19 89 are $1,200
Property Insurance $750/YR.   Association Fee
Natural Gas $740/YR Electricity $270/YR Other
Income from Rent or Additional Expenses

Style of Home Rambler
Year Built 1950   Total Square Feet 800

List of Rooms	Measurements	Features
Living Room	12' x 14'	Large Windows
Kitchen-Dining	10' x 12'	
Bedroom	10' x 10'	Corner Windows
Bedroom	10' x 12'	Walk-in Closet
Finished Basement		

Dishwasher (X)   Garbage Disposal (X).   Stove (X).   Refrigerator (X)
Microwave ( )   Washer ( )   Dryer ( )   Water Softener ( )
Type of Heat Gas   Air Conditioning ( )
Hot Water Gas   Water Softener ( )
Electrical 200 AMP

State of Kitchen: Good
State of Bathrooms: Good
Outdoors: Large Backyard with Paved Patio
Price and Financing I Would Offer: $67,000 - Assume $40,000
  Mortgage, $20,000 2nd mortgage from sellers, $7,000 cash.

STEP 5

PRICING—WHAT IT'S WORTH TO YOU

Tradition says, as a buyer, you will probably base the price you pay for a home on the amount the seller is asking. Step 5 will free you from that limiting tradition by teaching you how to:

- DISENGAGE THE ASKING PRICE
- PAY A PRICE BASED ON RESALE VALUE
- PAY A PRICE BASED ON THE POSSIBILITY OF RENTING
- PAY A PRICE BASED ON YOUR MONTHLY BUDGET
- KNOW HOW MUCH THE SELLERS WILL GET
- COMPARE PRICES OF HOMES SOLD
- PRACTICE PRICING

The first thing I'll show you about pricing a house is what *not* to do. Don't do what *is* done; it's what I call the tribal mating dance. It goes like this:

- The sellers decide the lowest price they would like to get for their home is $80,000. To this amount, as is the custom, they add a little. The asking price ends up at $90,000.

- The buyers want to buy the home and they are nudged on, "Go ahead, make an offer." Boldly, daringly, from the asking price of $90,000 they deduct a little. They offer $80,000.

- Wonder of wonders! The sellers accept. Wow! Those buyers got a steal!

Or did they get hornswoggled? Yes, of course, it was all a hoax, a play. The dance was a prearranged distraction. The buyers never noticed that free and open negotiations didn't cut in. The buyers and sellers had performed the perfect ritual. Each one acted as expected, resulting in the predictable outcome.

DISENGAGE THE ASKING PRICE

Free yourself from offering a price that is a percentage of the seller's asking price. Shelve the asking price. Forget about it. Pursue your reasons for paying *any* price. Ask yourself, "What's it worth to me?"

Q. What if the sellers are firm on what they'll accept? Won't we waste time thinking about what it's worth to us and making a low offer?

A. No, it is time well spent. Of course, when you get around to making an offer, you'll have to face up to what the sellers want. But before you do that, consider what is the best price for you. That means independently, without the influence of what the sellers want, decide what you want to pay.

Use a businesslike approach. Clearly, buying a home is more than a business, more than an investment. What you expect from a home isn't measured only in dollars and cents. But let's look at different approaches that can support reasons for paying a price. In the end, there's no one way. Usually, the matter of price is arrived at as a mixture of reasons and instincts.

PAY A PRICE BASED ON RESALE VALUE

Here is a tough test for the price you choose to offer. It's strictly for the overall picture. In life as we know it, buying a home for the short term—less than three to five years—is doomed to be costly. Figure the expenses of buying, add the agency fees, legal and financing fees, the costs of moving out of one place and into another, new furniture purchases, and decorating. When you have a total of every cost you can think of, add 10 percent for the unexpected expenses.

It's not a good bet that you'll recoup these expenses if you turn around and sell the house immediately. The reality of buying and having to sell is sobering. Maybe that's what makes it worth looking into.

My advice is *don't* buy if you think you'll move soon. *Do* pay a price so that if you must, you can sell tomorrow without losing your shirt.

A resale checklist:

These are six conditions that affect resale. The more of these conditions that apply to your home, the easier it will be to resell.

The Price You Pay makes yours the lowest-priced home sold on the block or in the condo project. This is old advice kept young because it works. With homes selling for between $80,000 and $100,000 try to pay less than $80,000—or surely not more. Then, if you have to turn around and resell, you can price the home in the low end of the range and still get your money out. Also, the lower the price of a home the more buyers there are who could buy it.

The Home Is in Move-in Condition Any added cost for remodeling or redecorating adds to the price. The price ends up being what you paid for the home plus what you paid for sprucing it up.

The Home Includes Big-Tag Household Conveniences Such as a stove, refrigerator, washer, dryer, carpets, and window treatments. A home requiring less extra cost to move into is more salable.

Pay No Real Estate Fees and No Up-front Costs of Financing Or pay as little for these services as possible. So, if the sellers are willing to accept $94,000, you pay $94,000. The idea is to eliminate, or narrow down as much as possible, the non-refundable costs of the transaction.

Your Financing Is Assumable by New Buyers at an Attractive Interest Rate This might be a mortgage you assumed from the sellers that can be assumed again or a new mortgage that can be assumed by the next buyers. An assumable mortgage, with a favorable interest rate, is convenient and less costly than new financing.

The Home Has Charm This sounds whimsical, but a home that charms you has something special about it that will charm another buyer, too.

PAY A PRICE BASED ON THE POSSIBILITY OF RENTING

You also can pay a price based on the possibility of renting.

Second homes are often bought with a view to renting them out when they are not being used by the owners. The one to talk to about renting a second home is your tax adviser. Rules apply to tax deductions that you should be aware of before you buy a second home with renting in mind. But the renting I'm talking about is when you rent your #1 home as a result of an emergency situation. What if you buy, have to move out of town, and can't sell?

Renting at such a time can be a life preserver in a stormy sea; something to hang onto until help arrives, a way to pay the bills until the home sells. Keep in mind that this is a survival tactic. Generally, the price you pay for a home today and what it could rent for makes renting the least desirable option if you have a choice. If you have no choice, renting is not a bad deal if the rent, at the very least, covers your expenses.

> **Q.** How do we know what a place like ours will rent for?
>
> **A.** Check with friends who rent in the area or own rental property. Look in the For Rent section of the classified ads. Telephone a local rental agency.

PAY A PRICE BASED ON YOUR MONTHLY BUDGET

Here is a safe way to determine a price you can afford to pay for a home.

How much does your budget allow you to spend each month for shelter? The worksheet on page 77 will help you answer that question.

> **Q.** Why should we bother to figure out what we would pay when it's up to the mortgage company as to how much we can borrow?
>
> **A.** For control and to know where you stand. Possibly to use financing other than from a mortgage lender such as seller financing.

KNOW HOW MUCH THE SELLERS WILL GET

> **Q.** Why is it so important to know the price the sellers get?
>
> **A.** Because the difference between what you pay and what sellers get—no matter where these costs are hidden—is money that you, the buyers, end up paying.
>
> You pay $85,000—sellers end up with $75,000 (from this they pay off their loan and keep the money left over for their equity). You have paid $85,000 because of real estate fees and up-front costs of financing.
>
> Once you buy, you're in the owner's shoes. Now you're the owner of a home you could expect to sell for $75,000.

You make a grave mistake if you fall into the trap of calling the difference between the price you pay and

WORKSHEET FOR PRICE BASED ON MONTHLY BUDGET

Our Gross Monthly Income:
(Include all salaries and interest on savings.)

$ __3,200__

25 percent of the above Gross Monthly Income:

$ __800__

Our monthly long-term debt payments total:
(Include all monthly payments of over six-month duration.)

$ __200__

You can safely take on a mortgage that has a monthly payment of not more than 25 percent of your Gross Monthly Income, *and*, when added to your existing long-term monthly payments, will not exceed 35 percent of your Gross Monthly Income.

the price sellers get as the cost of selling. This difference is the cost of buying!

Look closely—Who pays the price with the costs included? The buyers. Who has to try to recoup the costs when they sell? The buyers.

As one buyer put it, if you go to K mart and buy designer jeans at discount instead of paying full price at Bloomingdales, who doesn't pay the extra price? Who gets the savings? The buyer, of course. The same is true of a home—the buyers pay the costs or reap the savings.

COMPARE PRICES OF HOMES SOLD

When a home on which you have gathered the Vital Statistics sells, call the sellers and say, "I'm trying to get a feel for home prices in your area. Would you mind telling me what price your home sold for? And the financing?"

It's good advice not to totally trust the price sellers tell you. Ask the buyers, too. Asking both buyers and sellers, if you can, would be an ideal cross check.

The *true* price a home sells for is not always easy to uncover. Financing makes a difference. If buyers pay cash to the sellers, they'll get a lower price than if the sellers carry back a mortgage. So even finding out the selling price is not the whole picture. You need to know the financing.

The county registrar of documents has public records on sales filed. Call there and say, "I'm looking to buy a home in the Garden area. Could you help me find the price of homes sold there in the last year?" The local newspaper may also publish this information weekly. Real estate companies have a limited picture because they only know what they sold, not what owners sold. It's worth a call to ask.

But remember, you can never get a firm grip on housing prices like you can the closing price of IBM stock on Wall Street. You'll always make an offer wishing you had more information. It's the nature of home buying.

PRACTICE PRICING

Practice pricing when inside a home.

The skill of bargain pricing comes with practice. Try it every chance you get.

The best time to practice is while you're looking inside a home. While you are wrapped up in critically evaluating the home itself, bring your thoughts around to price evaluating. Be tough. Ask yourself, "At what price would I consider this home a good value?"

Write it down. On the bottom line of the home's Vital Statistics worksheet, fill in "Price and Financing I Would Offer for the Home."

Q. Wouldn't it be simpler to hire an appraiser to tell us the price to pay?

A. No. For homes, unlike investment property, an appraiser looks to the past—what others have paid for like property. You buy for the future. You want to pay a price influenced by what you see in *your* future.

STEP 6

BARGAINING

Knowing what you want, need, and can afford to buy in a home puts you in a powerful and positive position to bargain with sellers. In Step 6 I'll cover some ideas on how to:

- FIND OUT WHAT'S IMPORTANT TO THE SELLERS
- KNOW WHEN TO SPEND MORE THAN THE ASKING PRICE
- AVOID PRIOR RESTRAINT
- KEEP IN MIND BUYERS MAKE THEIR OWN BARGAINS
- BEWARE THE SELLERS' PRICE-SUPPORT SYSTEM
- MAKE AN OFFER
- DOs AND DON'Ts OF WINNING NEGOTIATIONS
- ACT ON SELLER'S RESPONSE

When you determine what a property is worth to you, it's time to calculate its worth to the sellers. Their asking price may be important, but other factors may be more important.

> **Q.** Won't sellers get mad if a buyer disregards the asking price and makes a low offer?
>
> **A.** Some may. Some may hate the price but love the offer. Some are relieved to have solved the problem of selling the home and get on with their lives.

FIND OUT WHAT'S IMPORTANT TO THE SELLERS

Consider Jan and Sonny, who wanted to buy a home with an asking price of $70,000. They took the time to look at the sale from the perspective of what was important to the seller and ended up buying the house for $53,835. (The terms of their offer are on the Offer Worksheet on page 84.)

Here's their story:
        Jan and Sonny learned what they could about the seller and figured his top priority was to get out from under his obligations on the home as soon as possible. They found out from friends down the street that the home had been for sale for almost a year. The owner had married and moved into his wife's home. The home Jan and Sonny wanted was empty.
        The financing was a good news/bad news situation. There was an assumable $45,000 mortgage with a low interest rate, but a big chunk of cash was required because there was a second mortgage of $7,000 due on sale. Also, a multiple listing agent was involved and would require a fee of more than $3,000. So, it looked like more than $10,000 in cash would be required just

to pay off the seller's obligations. Jan and Sonny did not have enough cash.

But by somehow providing the seller the cash he needed, they figured they could influence him to accept a low offer. Sonny's parents agreed and offered a second mortgage to loan Sonny and Jan the money they needed.

Next, they calculated and presented the lowest possible price they thought the seller would accept (next page). The real estate agent agreed to give the buyer's agent's discount. In fact, the agent sold the deal to the seller pointing out it was not the deal they were hoping for, but it would at least take the seller off the hook. It would pay what he owed, plus leave a little extra money for closing expenses.

Note the closing date on the Offer Worksheet. This date—only one month away—was a big reason the seller accepted the low offer. The fast closing was the cherry on the sundae—the chance to get out quickly.

When the terms of this offer are agreed to by all parties, buyers and sellers, the buyers will have a legally binding sales contract written and returned to the sellers for signatures. The sellers agree to hold the property until that date.

Price may be most important to some sellers, however.

"If I get my price," was the only condition under which Mrs. Evers, a widow, would sell. She had no reason to be in a hurry to move. She had the biggest back yard in the neighborhood. She would say, "Someone who loves the yard as I do will pay my price."

She was right. She refused several low offers. The people who finally bought the home started out with a low price. Mrs. Evers refused to lower her price until the third offer the buyers made. Then she only came down from $127,000 to $125,000.

As it turned out, the seller was right to hold her price. She had nothing pressing to get on to. She could wait.

The buyers played their hand well. They tried for a lower price. Tried three times. They loved the home,

---

OFFER WORKSHEET

For property as presented on the previous VITAL STATISTICS FORM.

DATE ___July 1, 1990___

A. PRICE OFFERED ___$55,500___

    LESS ANY BUYER'S AGENT'S DISCOUNT ___$1,665___
    For a FINAL PRICE of ___$53,835___

B. THE FINAL PRICE IS TO BE PAID SUBJECT TO
    OBTAINING FINANCING:
    First Mortgage in the amount of ___$45,000___
    with the following terms: ___Assumed from seller___

    Second Mortgage in the amount of _____
    with the following terms: _____

    CASH IN THE AMOUNT OF ___$8,835___
    FOR A TOTAL EQUAL TO THE FINAL
       PRICE ABOVE $ ___53,835___

C. ON THE CLOSING DATE ___August 1, 1990___

D. THIS OFFER EXPIRES ON ___July 5, 1990___
(If a legally binding sales contract is not signed by buyers and sellers on, or before, the above date, this offer expires.)

they wanted it. In making low offers they were diplomatic, careful not to leave hard feelings.

> **Q.** How do you find out what's important to sellers?

> **A.** Look several places. Ask the seller, "What are you looking for in the sale?" Ask around about the seller. Put yourself in the seller's shoes. What do you think the seller wants? Then try an offer and see how the seller responds. Keep trying, feeling your way.

WHEN TO SPEND MORE THAN THE ASKING PRICE

On a choice property, you may run into competition with other buyers. Here is where the work you did earlier in Step 5, Pricing: What It's Worth to You, pays off.

When you know ahead of time what a property is worth to you, you'll know your limit. If a seller says, "Two other buyers plan to make offers," you wont get caught in a bidding war. Offer as much as you figure the property is worth. Even if that is more than the asking price.

However, if your price doesn't match the asking price, watch out. Don't let the heat of competition carry you into offering a price you'll kick yourself for later.

> **Q.** Won't I kick myself if I miss getting a home I really want?

> **A.** Not if you keep looking. There are many homes you will fall in love with. Keep looking and I believe you'll find a home you love even more because the home you'll

love most is the one you buy at a price you can live with.

Q. But say we find a home we really love and the seller won't lower the price. Do you think we're foolish to stretch our budget for a home we feel is the "one and only"?

A. No. You may be wise to give up something in your budget to pay more for a home you love. Awareness makes the difference. Have your eyes wide open to what you are paying and how you'll make the payments. Then go for it.

AVOID PRIOR RESTRAINT

You are your own enemy bargaining if you are thinking the following:

"We'll hurt the seller's feelings."

"It's so much lower than their asking price."

"They'll never take it anyway. Why bother?"

If those are the things you are telling yourself, argue back:

"We'll never get it for less than we offer."

"We can always up the price."

"We'll never know unless we try."

Let's face it. If you make a low offer, you're taking your chances. But how can you know how sellers will respond when sellers don't know themselves? They know when it happens.

To one seller receiving a low offer is "shocking," to another it's "expected," to another it's "welcome."

Q. What if sellers turn down our low offer?

A. It's better that the sellers turn you down than to not make the offer. The one time you are sure not to get a low price is if you don't try. Besides, many sellers will make counter offers and leave the door open for you to continue to negotiate.

KEEP IN MIND BUYERS MAKE THEIR OWN BARGAINS

One real estate investor I know says, "The only time I control the price of a property is when I buy. Then I'm free to take it or walk away. But if I have to sell, I'm stuck. I have to take the best price a buyer offers."

An offer in writing, using the Offer Worksheet, is businesslike, emotion free, detached from hoopla. No matter how low the price, the offer calls for a reasonable response. Expect it.

BEWARE THE SELLERS' PRICE-SUPPORT SYSTEM

The "hard" evidence that sellers can use like weapons to defend their asking price sometimes overwhelms and intimidates buyers. Be prepared to let sellers' defenses roll off your back without compromising your position. Willingly, sellers will bring out appraisals, market-value estimates by real estate agents, computer printouts of homes sold in the neighborhood, and cost receipts of improvements that have been made.
Be prepared to attack as follows:

An Appraisal No matter how expert the appraiser, he or she can't put a price on your home. No one can ever understand all the factors that are important to you. An appraiser judges what's important to him or her.

Market-Value Estimate by a Real Estate Agent Giving free market evaluations is the way real estate agents get business. It's a device to butter up sellers and entice the sellers to "come list with me." As such, agents wanting to ingratiate the most give maximum, sometimes outrageously high, market-value prices.

Computer Printouts of Homes Sold in the Neighborhood Interesting. Worth looking over. Usually these lists are limited to homes sold by real estate companies, not by owners. Sometimes homes on the list are carefully selected to justify a higher price.

Cost Receipts of Improvements Made Again, interesting. But not necessarily suited to your needs. I know buyers who paid more for a home without the extra finished room. They didn't want to have to keep up the extra space.

> **Q.** Negotiating with a seller scares me. Should I give my offer to the listing agent or to my lawyer to handle for me?
>
> **A.** Neither. Never leave your offer in anyone's hands but your own. Take someone with you, if you wish. Make up your own negotiating team. But you be there to hear the seller's response. You look the seller in the eye. You decide what to do next. Practice

saying, "I don't know. I'll have to find that out. I'll have to give that some thought." You don't have to respond to everything on the spot. Stall if you need time.

Q. When do we apply for financing?

A. After the legal sales contract is written. The lender will insist on a copy of the contract before taking an application for a mortgage.

Q. Is there any way to know what the price should be?

A. There's no way. Keep in mind the basic rule for price: a price is what sellers will take and buyers will give for a particular product at one particular time.

The price and financing you offer exists only inside your head. I can't help you with that. I can, however, give you the following checklist to be sure you are ready to make an offer.

- Do you have in mind a home you love and a price you can live with?
- Have you looked at many homes so you can make valid comparisons?
- Do you have a completed Vital Statistics Form on each of the comparable homes?
- Do you have SOLD prices on similar homes?
- Have you claimed independence and the discount on the buyer's agent's fee if the property is multiple-listed?
- Do you know what the sellers need?

With a yes answer to each of the above questions, you're ready to make an offer. You've done the leg work and the head work. Now trust your good judgment.

MAKE AN OFFER

There are several ways to make an offer.

Real estate agents generally make an offer by completing a full, legal sales contract with the buyers. The contract is then presented to the sellers. If sellers accept the contract and sign it, the deal is binding.

I don't recommend buyers or sellers sign a sales contract without a lawyer.

You can write a sales contract on your own, although I don't recommend that either. You can go to a stationery store that sells legal documents. Ask for a standard real estate sales contract, purchase agreement, or whatever the contract is called in your area. You can fill in the blanks yourself and take it to the sellers. But this is hardly the time or the place for a do-it-yourself legal project. I don't recommend that you sign a legally binding contract on the biggest purchase of your life without a qualified legal adviser. Too many things can go wrong. To err may be human, but when you err with real estate it can be very expensive.

I recommend this:

1. You make an offer using the Offer Worksheet on page 84.
2. The sellers accept or do not accept the offer based on these items:
    — Price
    — Financing
    — Closing Date
    — Request for the Buyer's Agent's Fee Discount if the property is multiple-listed.

If the sellers say they accept the terms of the offer, it is considered the responsibility of you, the buyer, to arrange for a legally binding sales contract. Bring the Offer Worksheet to your lawyer or escrow or title agent who can use the terms of the Offer to construct a sales contract.

Q. Why, when you recommend not putting signatures on the Offer, is it better to make a written agreement rather than just sitting down and talking with the sellers?

A. The written offer is a stronger statement for the following reasons:

1. You state price, financing, date of closing, and request for buyer's agent's discount at the same time. There is a dramatic difference between saying you'll pay $70,000 in cash tomorrow and saying you'll pay it with a note to the sellers paid off in 30 years.
2. You state the information precisely. There can be no misunderstanding about the terms of the offer.
3. You can leave the offer on the bargaining table, walk away, and call the sellers later.
4. If the sellers want to make any changes or make a counter offer, they can cross off what you have written and add their changes.
5. You narrow the discussion to what's most important—the money and how and when you will pay it.
6. You keep away from delving into legal title and keep from paying for legal expertise until necessary.

7. If and when you do come to an agreement on the terms of the offer, you have the information you need clear and in writing. You're ready to have a sales contract written.

Q. How do the sellers know I have the income to pay for their place?

A. They might ask you where you work and how much you earn. You would be wise to tell them before they ask. Telling the sellers more about yourself than they ask is a nice way to lay the groundwork for your offer.

Add further conditions of the offer in writing.

In real estate, all dealings should be in writing and signed by all parties. If that's not a law everywhere, it's at least a well-accepted rule and good advice for you, the independent buyer. Having terms written in your Offer assures that whatever is agreed to is clear to both parties. It also assures that whatever is agreed to will be included in the final sales contract.

The sales contract becomes the rock upon which the sale is built. Make sure everything you want is stated there.

The Vital Statistics Form should state most of what is included with the home. Make sure that certain appliances, rugs and curtains you expect to be getting are listed in writing.

If anything beyond the actual land and building is to be included in the deal, write it on the Offer. For example, some second-home condominiums are sold "with all furniture."

DOs AND DON'Ts OF WINNING NEGOTIATIONS

DO give prime thought to how you'll make your offer to the sellers. Telephone ahead so they know you are coming with an offer. If you are on chatty terms with the sellers, sit with them at the kitchen table. Discuss your offer, listen to their response.

If you are more comfortable at arm's length, write the offer on the Offer Worksheet. When you arrive at the scheduled time, hand the sellers the offer. Say, "We love your home. The price we've come up with may be lower than you expect, but we can offer you a quick closing date (or the extra time they need before closing the deal, or whatever may be particularly important to the sellers). Please give it some thought. Sleep on it. We'll call you in the morning for your response."

DON'T be combative. To win, don't act like a winner. The prize is awarded for how you play the game. Don't try to "sell" a low price. Anything you say digs you deeper into the hole. It's best not to say too much. Listen. Remember you are trying to find out what the sellers need.

DO be positive. Set aside your negative reasons for a low offer. Say, "We both love to cook. We're planning to enlarge the kitchen."

DON'T put down the home. Don't say, "We both love to cook. We plan to enlarge the kitchen because we couldn't put up with your cramped space."

DO make good use of time. Allow time to talk it over, time for the shock of the offer to wear off, time for the good points to sink in, time for sellers to say, "These are nice people for our home, let's accept it. Let's get it behind us."

DON'T make the offer with "now or never" finality. Don't offer the choice of take it or leave it. Instead, give the feeling of "take it now or think about it and take it later." Time usually works in the buyer's favor.

> **Q.** Do you mean we should just leave the offer without a time limit?
>
> **A.** No. I mean time as in a day or maybe two. Be sure to fill in the space on the Offer form after, "This offer expires on _____."
>
> I learned to limit the time of any offer the hard way. Once, when I left an offer without a time limit, I couldn't reach the seller for more than a week. I found out later why he didn't return my calls. He was contacting all potential buyers who might be interested in buying his place for just a few dollars more than my offer. He was shopping the offer as the pros call it. He found another buyer. This is a low-life way of doing business, but it's done.

ACT ON SELLER'S RESPONSE

If the sellers accept, telephone your legal adviser for an appointment to meet to write a sales contract.

If the sellers flatly reject your offer, ask them to respond with a counter offer. That means to cross out what they can't accept and write in what suits them. Or give them a spare Offer Worksheet to counter your offer.

If sellers counter your offer, accept it or counter it again, DON'T REJECT IT. Come back with something even if it's only a couple dollars more than your previous offer. If you're really interested in the property, keep the ball in the air.

Negotiations can become a tennis match. The offer moves back and forth between the buyers and sellers. The reason I say keep it going is this: You never know how close sellers are to saying "OK." Maybe this counter offer of just a few more dollars will convince sellers to accept.

When the offer is agreed to, get to work on a sales contract and get a commitment on financing. To do this, move on to Step 7: Closing the Deal.

STEP 7

CLOSING THE DEAL

You've struck a deal to buy a home you want at the price you want, but to properly protect your investment you'll need legal and financial help. In Step 7 I'll share some thoughts about completing the sale and tell you how to:

- GO DIRECTLY TO YOUR LEGAL ADVISER
- STATE FIRMLY AND FULLY ALL TERMS OF THE SALE ON THE SALES CONTRACT
- HAVE SELLERS SIGN
- PICK A LENDER AND GET A COMMITMENT ON A LOAN
- FALTER NOT IN YOUR PURSUIT
- DOs AND DON'Ts WHEN PREPARING TO CLOSE
- COMPLETE THE BUYER'S STATEMENT
- LEARN BASIC LEGAL WORDS

If you've never bought a house before, expect to feel a letdown of spirits at this point in the buying process. It happens most to first-time buyers. Don't be surprised if you hear yourself saying, "What have we done?" After all, you've taken a big step in your life. It's a 10-point psychological jolt on a 10-point scale.

Step 7 in the independent buying process is crucial and needs your immediate and concentrated attention. You now need a legal adviser to:

- Write a sales contract
- Hold the earnest money
- Oversee the closing, the legal transfer of ownership

State laws vary. Ask your mortgage lender which legal person transfers real estate title between buyer and seller. Your legal person may be a lawyer, escrow-company agent, or a title-company agent.

Q. What will a legal person charge to write a sales contract, hold the earnest money, and oversee the closing?

A. Usually $300 to $500, but spell out your needs and ask your adviser for an estimate.

Q. If the seller has a real estate agent, can't this agent take care of my needs, too?

A. No. The agent may take care of the closing, but have a legal expert look after your best interest in the transaction by reading over the documents.

GO DIRECTLY TO YOUR LEGAL ADVISER

To write the sales contract, call your legal adviser for an appointment. Have your adviser write the contract with you in the office. After the sales contract is signed, all business with your lawyer can be conducted by phone or mail. This saves the lawyer's time and your money.

Getting the sales contract written well cements a good bond between buyers and sellers and makes it easier to proceed to closing. The legal adviser may write the contract from scratch or use a standard form that is available in most stationery stores that carry legal documents.

Q. Why do I need legal expertise?

A. Even when a buyer works with a real estate agent, I recommend employing a legal expert at this stage. An agent, by license, can bring together buyers and sellers and help them come to agreement on a price. But giving legal advice is out of bounds for an agent—strictly a "no-no." Remember the old-timer's advice: *If someone says you don't need a lawyer, run—don't walk—to the nearest lawyer.*

There is a maze of constantly changing laws on home ownership. Laws differ in different states and in counties and cities within states. A lawyer once told me that when there are lots of laws on a subject it's because there have been lots of conflicts over it. Based on my experience, if that's true, the legal history of home ownership must read like *War and Peace*.

I recommend working with legal experts because, in many ways, as a buyer you are a gambler. You are buying the future. When the deal closes you are left with all the risks. When all the papers are signed:

- The sellers walk away with your money.

- The lender walks away with a claim to the home for which you just went in debt and for which you probably scraped together all your savings.

- You're left with a lapful of obligations:

  - The obligation to pay back the biggest debt in your life.

  - The obligation to pay property taxes.

  - The obligation to pay gas and electric bills.

  - The obligation to keep up the physical property or watch it deteriorate.

  - The obligation to protect yourself with insurance from loss by fire or injury to another person on your property and a possible lawsuit.

  - The obligation to have invested your money wisely.

  - The obligation to make owning a home a happy time.

If you think you can take all this on without being on firm legal footing, you're too trusting to be let out of the house alone.

Q. What can a lawyer do?

A. A lawyer can guide you through this legal maze with an eye to preventing future problems and assure you that:

1. The property you get is what you expect.

2. If the property is a town house, condo, or co-op, you need to request and receive legal documents from the property association with time to review them.

3. The financing has no unexpected demands—like a balloon payment or penalty for paying off the mortgage early.

4. The passing of title follows local laws.

5. The title is clear, one that you can sell when the time comes.

6. You take title under the name and entity that best protects you. I refer here to Joint Tenancy or Tenants in Common.

STATE FIRMLY AND FULLY ALL TERMS OF THE SALE ON THE SALES CONTRACT

Q. How binding is a sales contract that is properly written and signed?

A. Very. If you change your mind and the sellers won't agree to cancel, you can be required to go through with the sale. I know of a business executive in Hawaii who signed a sales contract for a $1 million home on the ocean. The day before the closing he was transferred to the mainland. Advised by his lawyer that he could be sued and forced to buy the property, he went ahead and bought it and listed it for sale the same day.

Q. If the property we're buying is multiple-listed, should our claim to self-representation and the Request for Buyer's Agent's Fee Discount be stated in the sales contract?

A. Yes. Bring along to your legal adviser a copy of the Request for Buyer's Agent's Fee Discount form in order that it can be stated fully in the sales contract.

It is hoped that with a well-thought-out sales contract, your deal will proceed smoothly to closing. Some of the items the contract will include:

1. *Price and Financing.* If you plan to apply for a new mortgage, you'll do that after the sales contract is signed by all the buyers and sellers.

   You apply for financing following a firm sales contract because lenders want to be sure you have a firm commitment from the sellers—to sell at a set price—before going to the trouble of deciding to lend you the money.

   Important Note: Make sure your sales contract is worded so that your price is contingent upon getting specific financing. If the contract states that you will pay $80,000, subject to obtaining a $70,000 mortgage to be paid over 30 years at a 10 percent interest rate, but the lender won't give a mortgage for less than 10.5 percent, you are not obligated to complete the purchase. The deal falls through and you are free to renegotiate.

2. *Settlement or Closing Date.* The date is important because it puts everyone on a time schedule. However, missing the date for an innocent reason—because say the lender isn't ready—doesn't cancel the contract. Legal minds have come to the conclusion that the closing date is a target date. If the date is missed, the contract isn't canceled. Everyone reschedules.

Q. Can a contract be canceled?

A. Yes and no. If all signers to the contract agree, there is usually no problem. It's when one signer wants to cancel and another doesn't that you run into problems. Under any circumstance, it takes a cancellation document. Call upon your legal adviser.

3. *Request for Buyer's Agent's Fee Discount.* if the property is multiple-listed. Refuse to sign unless the sales contract states: *Since there is no buyer's agent, the seller's agent agrees to reduce the obligation of the seller to pay the real estate fee by the amount usually paid to the buyer's agent.*

4. *Request Town House, Condo, or Co-op Association Documents.* if the property is one of these types. Usually the request is tied in with the right for the buyer to cancel any time during a 15-day period while reviewing the documents.

5. *Earnest Money.* The amount of earnest money that goes along with the sales contract. This is a substantial amount of money. It must show your sincerity to go through with the contract. It's necessary for sellers to have this sign of commitment from buyers. After all, sellers are expected to take their home off the market. They want a little security that indeed a sale will follow.

   Discuss with your lawyer who will be selected to hold the earnest money. It could be put into a lawyer's trust account, an escrow, or title company. In any case, it will be somewhere that both buyer and seller agree to.

   A word here about earnest money. It will be in limbo, no man's land, until the deal closes

or falls through. If the deal falls through because the buyers can't get the specified financing, the buyers get back the earnest money. If
the buyers and the sellers agree to cancel the
sales contract, the buyers and the sellers decide what to do with the money. Disposition
of earnest money due to other reasons for
canceling must be decided—usually with the
help of legal advisers—on an individual basis.
Sellers can say, "We incurred a delay in selling
because of this offer. We want the earnest
money to pay what we lost." So, know when
you write the check that if you default, you
could lose that money.

HAVE SELLERS SIGN

Make sure you understand the large and small print on
the sales contract and agree with everything before
signing it.

Return to the sellers with the contract for their signature. Don't be surprised if the sellers are ready to
sign the contract as it is. They may not feel a need for
a legal adviser. If, however, they are going to hold a
mortgage on the property, they'll want help—if they
don't they should.

If the sellers are married, be sure both sign. If one
of the sellers is out to town, ask your lawyer how to
get the signature so the commitment is legal. There are
different ways to do it, but usually sending a telegram
of acceptance isn't enough. An actual signature usually
is required. You may have to send the actual documents or duplicates by overnight mail.

Q. When will the sellers move out?

A. Usually on the same day they pass title to
you, they also pass along the keys for you to

take possession. It takes approximately six weeks from the day the sales contract is signed until buyers can take possession—it takes that long for financing to be arranged and legal title examined—but it could be shorter or longer.

If there is a disagreement with the sellers about something on the sales contract, chances are it will be about some item of personal property. Remember:

- Try to be reasonable.
- Keep your perspective as to value.

Both sides—buyers and sellers—can become irrational about leaving personal items in a home. Believe it or not, I once handled a $250,000 sale that almost fell through because of a disagreement over a plastic shower curtain.

If you run into a disagreement keep cool, be reasonable, be polite, and take your time. Say "I don't know." If a legal question comes up, call your lawyer or escrow or title agent.

PICK A LENDER AND GET A COMMITMENT ON A LOAN

It's in Step 7 that your leg work searching out lenders finally pays off. Take out your mortgage comparison worksheets. Chances are you have been following the local mortgage market as you've been looking for homes. Don't expect that what you hear about mortgage rates on the national news will always apply to you. Pockets of areas in the country can have drastically different climates for mortgages at any one time.

Call the lenders on your worksheet. You now have a specific amount of money you want to borrow, so ask a loan officer for specific current terms. Ask questions when you don't understand. Record it all. Choose the deal that's best for you.

> **Q.** There is a bank in the neighborhood where we are buying. It's a bank we don't have on our list. Should we call them about a mortgage since they are in the neighborhood?
>
> **A.** Yes. That's a worthwhile idea. Sometimes lenders like local business and will offer something special to homeowners in the neighborhood. Also check the bank where you do your other business, and the lender where the sellers' mortgage is presently held. They may do special favors for old customers.

Get a commitment from a lender.

After you apply for a loan, the lender will usually take a few weeks before giving approval. The home will be appraised. Is it worth the amount you are asking to borrow? You will be appraised. Do you work where you say you do, earn the money you say you earn? Do your references report that you are of sterling character?

Then, with all their questions answered, the lender will give approval or not. Either way, notify the sellers immediately and notify your legal adviser, who can now prepare closing documents.

FALTER NOT IN YOUR PURSUIT

If you get turned down for a mortgage by one lender don't give up. If you want the home, persistence counts here as anywhere. Consider the options that could affect your status with a lender. Why were you turned down? Can you come up with a little more down payment? Pay off an old loan? Think of options and alternative financing. Look in local classified ads for private lenders. Ask your lawyer if there are small companies who invest retirement funds in mortgages. Advertise in the classified ads for a lender—Wanted: private mortgage, $50,000 at 10 percent, good credit rating.

Do keep up the care, consideration, and courtesy you've practiced throughout the process so far. And add cleverness. Don't take off the velvet gloves or your stomping shoes.

DOs AND DON'Ts WHEN PREPARING TO CLOSE

DO   understand what you will be expected to sign.

DON'T   assume anyone looks out for you but yourself and your lawyer—mostly yourself.

DO ask to have copies of documents you'll be expected to sign a few days before closing so that you can read them thoroughly. If you're told this is not the practice, insist on it.

DON'T   sign documents you see for the first time at the closing unless you have time to read them carefully.

DO   ask questions, even if everyone else acts like they know everything. Maybe they do, but more likely they don't.

DON'T   be bashful. It's your money paying for all this.

DO know everything that's going on. Make sure it meets with your approval.

DON'T sign anything, especially checks, until you approve everything. You have the power to release the mortgage money with your signature. You are the star of the show. Keep control.

> **Q.** A lawyer will be our legal adviser when we buy our home independently. Do we need our lawyer at the closing?
>
> **A.** Not if your lawyer has had the documents ahead of time to review, make any changes, and give you the OK to sign. But make sure you have the lawyer's phone number in your pocket. And arrange that the lawyer or an associate will be available by phone in case a question arises.

Having the lawyer's approval before the closing is a good reason to insist on the documents a few days before the closing. This will save on the lawyer's time that you are charged for. Also, the closing is less likely to drag on with unexpected surprises.

COMPLETE THE BUYER'S STATEMENT

On the following page is a worksheet, an accounting of all the money you pay for a home. Fill in the numbers for the total price of your home.

The bottom-line price should make you a proud, happy, and financially satisfied homeowner. It should tell you that your independence allowed you to *Buy More Home for Less Money.*

BUYER'S STATEMENT

PRICE PAID TO SELLERS $70,000

Paid as follows:
Cash $7,000
Mortgage $63,000
Other   _____
Total $70,000
(Total must equal above price)

ADDITIONAL EXPENSES

Financing:
Points $900
Lender's Fee $1,200
Other $300

Lawyer $300

Government Fees $25

Escrow Fees $150

Advertising $40

Total Additional Expenses $2,915

Price Paid to Sellers plus
Total Additional Expenses $72,915
equal Price of Home

LEARN BASIC LEGAL WORDS

Abstract of Title A chronicled history of all recorded documents—such as title holders, loans, liens, death and marriage certificates—affecting ownership of a property.

Cancellation Document A written statement that cancels a written sales contract. It could simply state, "This is to cancel sales contract between (names of buyers) and (names of sellers) for property at (address)." It must be dated and signed by all parties who signed the sales contract.

Closing or Settlement or Closing Escrow A meeting at a specified time and place to finalize the sale. With a neutral party in charge—usually called a closer—all documents and checks get signed and distributed. Old debts get paid. Home expenses such as utility bills, taxes, rents, and management fees are prorated as specified in the sales contract. Further:

Buyers:

1. Sign a promissory note for the new money borrowed.
2. With a certified check, pay the remainder of the down payment (in addition to the earnest money paid at the sales contract signing).
3. Accept the deed from sellers conveying title to the property. If there is a Trust Deed, or a mortgage requires it, pass the deed to the lender or third party.

Sellers:

1. Pay money owed for fees, mortgages, loans, liens, and all other money demands.
2. Sign deed conveying title.
3. Take for themselves all money and any promissory notes from buyers left after the sellers' debts against the home are paid.

Contract for Deed or Land Contract or Contract of Sale An agreement between buyers and sellers allowing the sellers to withhold conveying the deed until buyers have met certain conditions and have paid certain amounts of money.

Deed A document that moves the title (ownership) from one party to another. It is not the title but it is one evidence of the title.

Quitclaim Deed The grantor gives up all rights whatever they may be.

Trust Deed A manner of securing the mortgage on a property whereby the deed is held by a third party (trustee).

Warranty Deed Refers to a guarantee of the condition of the title, not the condition of the home structure or the working conditions of anything inside the home such as the heating or electric systems. Guarantees that the title is free from all encumbrances.

Earnest Money A monetary deposit held by a third party—a lawyer or escrow or title agent—giving evidence of a buyer's sincerity when signing a sales contract.

Easement The right of one party to use land of another for a specific purpose.

Escrow Holding by a neutral third party.

1. A mortgage can call for monthly payments to include funds to be held for annual payment of property taxes and/or insurance.
2. A sales contract can call for funds, documents and instructions to be held for the closing on a property.

Escrow Agent An impartial person who holds documents, money, and instructions for a sales transaction for the buyer and the seller.

Fee Simple Commonly used to mean that the owner of a home also has title to the land rather than leasing the land.

Joint Tenancy Means that where there is more than one owner of a property, each owns equal shares and has equal right of possession. (Different from Tenants in Common.) When one owner dies, those shares pass immediately and equally to the surviving owners or owner.

Legal Description Locates the home in county records.

Lien A claim or hold of one person on the property of another to secure payment of a debt or obligation. The intent is that property can't be sold, and the owners walk away with the money, without paying the debt.

Marketable Title A title that is for all practical purposes clear, and one that a prudent buyer of real estate would accept.

Personal Property Possessions in a home easily moved, such as a free-standing refrigerator, washer, or dryer. They do not stay with the home unless specifically mentioned in the sales contract.

Possession Date Moving day when the sellers move out and the buyers move in. When this date is the same as closing date it is hectic but the best protection from future hassles.

Property Taxes Levied locally by city, county, or state. The amount is usually determined by the size and location of the home.

Purchase Agreement or Sales Contract A legal document between buyers and sellers stating their intentions and conditions to finalize a sale.

Real Property Everything built into the home and part of the home sale.

Sales Contract or Purchase Agreement Legal document between buyers and sellers stating their intention and conditions for finalizing a sale.

Tenancy in Common Means that where there is more than one owner on a property, each owns a separate share. (Different from Joint Tenancy.) When one owner dies, the share owned passes to that person's heirs.

Title Legally a very confusing concept. Commonly used interchangeably with the right to ownership. But you really don't own land in the same way that you own a car or shares of stock. With land you have the right or title to use it. Evidence of the right usually comes from the Deed.

Title Insurance A policy against defects in the title that don't show up immediately in the title search. Mortgage lenders often insist on it. Buyers pay for it.

Title Search An examination of public records to reveal the state of ownership on a property.

Torrens Refers to the Torrens System, a way to record land. Each property has its records in one document after the court establishes that the title is clear. In this document all matters affecting ownership, such as mortgages and liens, are recorded. Each time there is a new owner, the new name is recorded in the document and a copy given to the new owners. This copy is called the Owners Duplicate Certificate.